Molière

THE MAN SEEN THROUGH THE PLAYS

by

RAMON FERNANDEZ

Translated from the French

by

WILSON FOLLETT

 HILL AND WANG – NEW YORK

Copyright © 1958 by Hill and Wang, Inc.
Translated from the French, *La Vie de Molière*

The Library of Congress has cataloged this book as follows:

Fernandez, Ramon, 1894-1944.
  Molière: the man seen through the plays. Translated from the French by Wilson Follett. New York, Hill and Wang ₍1958₎
  212 p. 19 cm.
  Translation of La vie de Molière.

  1. Molière, Jean Baptiste Poquelin, 1622-1673.

PQ1852.F413   928.4   58-14200 ‡
Library of Congress

Manufactured in the United States of America
by The Colonial Press Inc.

To that great friend of Molière, Jacques Copeau

R. F.

To Mr. Jacques Le Clercq and to Mr. and Mrs. Henri Brugmans, publisher and translator make grateful acknowledgment for painstaking and valuable counsel about many textual details. These generous advisers are, however, in no smallest degree answerable for any defects that may be found to have survived their good offices.

CONTENTS

PREFACE

In the following pages I have attempted a biography somewhat apart from the common run. The subject is one to which I am drawn. The life of Molière is the life of his work; it is one vital aspect of the genius of comedy and of the French theater. Documents that can rightly be called biographical are extremely scarce, and several even of these are disputed. But Molière's comedies can enlighten us about what is of the first importance in connection with a man of his stature: the responses that he made to life, the drama and the purport of his career. Molière's history is a privileged one. Lack of data about the man throws us back upon his works and challenges us to tighten beyond the usual practice the affiliation of criticism with biography. Is it possible to rediscover the man through the work? Is it possible to understand how the outline of a life coincides with the curve of a profession? It is for the reader to decide whether this book holds satisfying answers to these problems. I wish it may, not so much that my own vanity may be gratified as that other biographers may be encouraged to direct their explorations toward the enigma of creativity.

R. F.

CHAPTER ONE

POINT OF DEPARTURE

JEAN POQUELIN, son of parents who lived in the Rue Saint Honoré, was baptized in the church of Saint Eustache on January 15, 1622. He was probably the oldest of six children, two of whom died shortly after birth. He was called Jean Baptiste by way of distinguishing him from a younger brother likewise christened Jean.

He was descended from a Beauvais family, one branch of which had settled in Paris toward the close of the sixteenth century. Here it conducted a retail upholstery business. Jean Poquelin, the father of our subject, married young Marie Cressé the year before Jean Baptiste's birth. She was the daughter of Louis Cressé, retail upholsterer and Paris burgher. Those who set store by hereditary influences will be gratified to learn that Molière's grandmother belonged to a family of court violinists.

The Paris Poquelins were typical of the rising bourgeoisie, which was characterized by unpretentious beginnings, occupations passed on from fathers to sons, steadily mounting incomes, and attainment of middle-class solidity. People of this class kept forging ahead without change of objective, always aware of new fields to conquer, and they never failed to buy at the first opportunity some public post related to their occupation. Monsieur Poquelin got his brother Nicolas to make over to him in 1631 the position of upholsterer-in-ordinary to the king.

Monsieur Poquelin was becoming a person of consequence. In 1647 we find him juryman and warden of the Paris guild of retail upholsterers, and he turns up among the appraisers entrusted with inventorying some of the furnishings of the royal household. His position was bringing him into proximity to the king. We visualize him in the royal bedchamber making up

the bed or, at the least, standing by at its foot to give
the *valets de chambre* a hand. An adroit salesman who
knows his rugs the way Monsieur Jourdain's father
knows cloth, he recruits customers among the personages thus informally encountered. It was not long
before Monsieur Poquelin could enter various celebrated names in his ledger—sometimes to his discomfiture, as when Monsieur de Cossé let his bill run for
ten years and, even then, beat his creditor down. But
Poquelin understood how to protect himself and how
to enforce his self-protection legally; against all
Dorantes he obtained court judgments. A man who
knew his way about, Monsieur Poquelin. Part of his
competence he accumulated by exploiting his success
as a money-maker with short- and long-term loans,
securing himself as needed with writs, judgments, and
attachments. He had a knack of making people take
an interest in him and of winning their trust. After
obtaining from his brother, in the interest of his son
Jean Baptiste, the post of upholsterer to the king, he
received by deed of gift his sister's holdings in real
estate, and when his daughter Catherine became a nun
he kept possession of the house in the business district
that she had inherited from her mother. When one of
his sons-in-law, having become a widower, set out on
prolonged travels he entrusted the management of his
affairs to Poquelin. Just as he had managed to provide
for his family and eke out his children's dowries,
Poquelin managed to arrange and safeguard his retirement. At the time of his making over his stock in
trade to his son, the younger Jean, he also rented him
his market place house, kept a bedroom in it for himself, and got his own right recognized to use kitchen
and cellarage and to go through the shop at will.

A systematic, consistent, and precise man, Monsieur
Poquelin seems to have been a benign father and a
generous one. When Jean Baptiste threw everything
overboard to go on the stage, there appears to have
been no inordinate exhibition of paternal rage. Molière
several times turned to his father for financial help,

and he got it, not without conditions. Jean Baptiste Poquelin ultimately achieved a theatrical career at once dazzling and respectable, and he did it by carrying on to the stage the spirit and the traditions of his family. But he could not accomplish this feat short of lifting comedy to the height that we can now appreciate, and that only with the astute help of a ruler who had wrought a good many changes in his kingdom. When Jean Baptiste turned actor there was no way on earth of foreseeing these consummations. He was simply putting an abrupt end to a rising curve, throwing everything to the winds, and making a fool of himself. It was a good thing that he had a brother.

Jean Baptiste's mother died very young, when he was nine, undoubtedly of a pulmonary trouble of the sort that was to end his own life at not far from fifty. She seems to have performed her duties with dignity and perhaps with sweetness. She knew how to read and write; she busied herself with the care of her household. Otherwise nothing is known about her. We know next to nothing about Jean Poquelin's second wife, Catherine Fleurette, whom he married the following year and who shortly died. We know hardly more about Jean Baptiste's maternal grandfather, who is said to have had an ardent addiction to the theater and to have taken his grandson to Hôtel de Bourgogne performances.

The Poquelins had two boxes and half of another in the roofed market hall of Saint Germain des Prés; Jean Baptiste's aunt had inherited them from her father. There were probably times when the child was taken to the Saint Germain fair and allowed to gape at the mountebanks and jugglers. Molière's works owe a good deal to farce, and specifically to French farce, already infiltrated by Italian; they owe it a good deal of their saltiness and even elements of their structure. The struttings and capers of Orviétan, the creaking of the stage, the mingled smells of the fair, and particularly the unearthly remoteness of the clowns, who seemed to have their being in a world apart, must have made a powerful impression on the youngster. We must not forget, however, that Jean Baptiste, when presently he dedicated himself to the theater, did not go in for the buffoon's craft. His own bent was toward tragedy. The Hôtel de Bourgogne, if he was actually taken there, must have wrought more decisively upon him than the fair did. And he was shortly to be exposed to influences even more persistent and more peremptory.

Monsieur Poquelin, intent on seeing his family come up in the world, was resolved that Jean Baptiste should enjoy the advantages that he himself had missed. He meant the boy to have a broad fundamental education, and to this end he turned to a famous institution, the College of Clermont, then on the site of the present Lycée Louis le Grand.

Clermont, administered by the Jesuit order, had a program of instruction different from that of its neighbor the University. It taught, besides the theology of the order, mathematics, physics, chemistry, dancing, and fencing. Awards of prizes were prefaced by the performance of tragedies and ballets composed by the reverend fathers and acted or danced by the students after painstaking rehearsals. The Jesuits were doing their utmost to turn out a rounded product and a man of character. Just what the Clermont of the seventeenth century stood for can be approximated if we think of sundry private schools of our day that teach the heirs of wealth to administer their property to good advantage. What Monsieur Poquelin aspired to is clearly enough indicated by his choice of Clermont.

Some degree of class distinction obtained among the students. A scion of the aristocracy had his own servant, his own tutor, and his own private bedroom. La Grange states that Jean Baptiste attended all his classes in the company of the Prince de Conti, who was later to be his patron and later still his calumniator. But the Prince de Conti was seven and a half years younger than Jean Baptiste. It can be presumed that the two were acquainted at the college and that the young prince's enthusiasm for the theater was one factor that drew them together. For it is extremely likely that the shows put on by the reverend fathers provided young Poquelin with the means of discovering his vocation. The Jesuits did more than the mountebanks to impel him stageward.

All Molière's biographers agree that he was a superior classical scholar, but their actual knowledge on this point is nil. All that a few general statements and commendations of him entitle us to believe is that he was a respectable student without being a conspicuously brilliant one. He knew Latin thoroughly, because it had been taught him thoroughly. He could read with fluency a comedy of Plautus or of Terence. As for the translation of Lucretius on which he is said to have worked all his life, those who were acquainted with it admired primarily its poetic style and its comprehension of the thoughts. It is my belief that Molière's own observation and ready intuition were always more important to him than book learning; that the expressiveness of his dialogue owed a much greater debt to his auditory than to his literary memory. In any event he acquitted himself creditably in his studies, and his father did not have to deplore the cost of his five or six years' attendance at an exclusive college.

Jean Baptiste had as fellow students Hesnault, who was a friend of the minister of finance, Fouquet; Bernier, who was to become physician to Aurangzeb the Mogul emperor; and Chapelle, illegitimate son of the comptroller, Luillier. The Provençal philosopher Gassendi was living in Luillier's house; the two were close friends. Gassendi, abreast of the accomplishments of recent physics, was pitting Galileo and Kepler against Aristotle; he was also working on his defense of Epicurus. He was a searching and a sharp thinker—sharp in every sense of the word—and master of a resourceful and formidable dialectic. It is asserted that he was giving regular instruction to

Chapelle and his friends, among them Bernier and Molière. It is even asserted that Cyrano de Bergerac the sham Gascon, though much older than the others, was privileged to attend these special classes. It is also recorded that Cyrano's play *Le Pédant Joué* was written in collaboration with Molière, and that Molière later reclaimed two scenes of his own invention for *Les Fourberies de Scapin;* whence his famous manifesto, "I take my own wherever I find it." This is, in any event, a tale that harms no one.

It is now considered disproved that Molière was Gassendi's pupil. However that may be, I believe that he was influenced by the philosopher, if but indirectly. The Gassendi of those years was a sort of unofficial instructor who left a deep impress on many minds. Bernier was an earnest Gassendist. Chapelle very soon went beyond his preceptor by espousing a vulgarized epicureanism to which some temperaments are predestined. But the influence that Gassendi exerted sprang less from the central purport of his teachings than from a particular bent for intellectual independence that he imparted to his students, an inclination toward free inquiry and scientific concepts. And his students imparted it in turn to their friends. Molière's addiction to Lucretius is extremely revealing of his predilections. In no wise a philosopher in the technical sense and indeed oblivious of certain spiritual realities, Molière nevertheless had an appetite for ideas and found infinite contentment in the use of his mind.

Jean Baptiste matriculated in law in 1641. The study of law, which had remained static ever since its reform under Henri IV, was taken very casually. There was no established minimum duration for it, no obligation to attend lectures. Things reached a point at which students were getting their examinations passed and their theses written by proxies. The professors were driving a trade in examination papers and refusing to do anything about replacing deceased colleagues. In 1651 the dean of the law faculty became the only professor left, and the University had to

petition the Parliament of Paris to compel him to
provide himself with colleagues. Such was the state
of affairs when Jean Baptiste took his degree at
Orléans, after letting one semester of study suffice,
as others did—possibly even less. Critics have called
attention to the exhaustive familiarity with legal procedure revealed in *Pourceaugnac*, *Les Fourberies de
Scapin*, and *L'École des Femmes*, but if they would
consult our journalists on the art of making a little
knowledge go far, they would concede that a hand-
book and five minutes' reading will very effectively
do duty for intensive study.

About this time—in 1642, from January 27 to July
23—Jean Baptiste was acting as substitute for his
father as upholsterer to the king. Louis XIII was then
at Narbonne. That young Poquelin actually went on
this trip seems to be corroborated by the fact that his
father was not out of Paris at all during that year.
The king, when he was making a long journey, slept
in his own bed at the end of each day's stage. It was
therefore necessary to have a duplicate set of furnishings. Each morning while one of the staff was having
the contents of the king's bedroom disassembled and
sent ahead, one of his colleagues, who had covered
the next day's stage, was getting everything ready
for the sovereign's arrival. Jean Baptiste was undoubtedly with Louis XIII at the siege of Perpignan,
and it is conceivable that he was present at the arrest
of the king's favorite, Cinq-Mars the master of the
horse, which occurred at Narbonne June 16. Legend
would have it that Jean Baptiste, in the capacity of an
anonymous young *valet de chambre*, made an effort
to rescue Cinq-Mars, but that is only a beguiling invention. It is more to the purpose to remember that
as Jean Baptiste, an official of the king, he traversed
the very region that was soon to become, as it would
long remain, the scene of his apprenticeship as
Molière.

Apparently Jean Baptiste was already acquainted
with the Béjarts, though we do not know exactly

when he formed his alliance with Madeleine Béjart. There were ten Béjart offspring, nominally controlled by a court usher father and an extremely unexacting mother. At least five of the ten went on the stage. They were an odd tribe, with a suggestion of the jailbird about them, yet with a place in both the lower middle class and the world of itinerant actors. The most gifted of the lot was Madeleine, an independent daughter who did not live under her mother's roof. She had one or two original tragedies to her credit, and La Grange's *Registre* informs us that on occasion she "doctored" others. As a poetess she had addressed some lines to Rotrou about his *Hercule Mourant*, and Rotrou had printed them. She was four years older than Molière. The understanding between them appears to have been both sudden and fundamental. Madeleine, a level-headed and resourceful woman with an eminent talent for business, gave Molière decisive help toward the building of his fortune. There was doubtless a sexual as well as a mental affinity. Molière was of an exceedingly amorous disposition, and Madeleine was no niggardly giver of herself. About this period she was the mistress of a singular personage known as Messire Esprit-Raymond de Moirmoron, Comte de Modène; he was chamberlain to the Duc d'Orléans, only brother of the king. A man of both pen and sword, more or less of an adventurer, he had been summed up by the Abbé Arnauld as "beyond question a man of merit, had he not vitiated in debauchery his admirable intellectual qualities" and as "a maker of as fine verses as any man in France." Madeleine had had a daughter by him in 1638. Aware that Madame de Modène was ill, she could cling for a long time to an expectation of becoming the Comte's wife. He did not gratify that expectation, but he did continue to be his mistress's friend as long as he lived. In 1640 Monsieur de Modène, becoming involved in a conspiracy against Louis XIII, came under sentence of death and fled to Brussels for asylum. Madeleine, who had already done some acting, must have resumed that occupation at just the time when Jean Baptiste was traveling through Roussillon.

The Béjarts, as we have seen, were a family that belonged half to the theater. The father, usher and court crier at the Bureau of Waters and Forests, was legally entitled to the cognomen "Sieur de Belleville," which smells of the actor. Since his wife had been, at Étampes, godmother to the son of Jean Baptiste Tristan L'Hermite, it has been inferred that she and Tristan L'Hermite were comembers of an itinerant troupe, a theory otherwise unsubstantiated. Madeleine had a commanding carriage and was a very good tragic actress. All this constituted a powerful enough appeal to fire Jean Baptiste, who already had a strong inclination. On January 6, 1643 he received from his father the sum of 630 livres, for which he relinquished his privileges as upholsterer *valet de chambre* to the king. Tradition has it that Jean Baptiste organized to begin with, along with several "youngsters of background," an amateur troupe that acted plays without charging admission. However that may be, it was not long before they were deriving revenue from their performances. The company included, besides Jean Baptiste, Denys Bey, Madeleine and Geneviève and Joseph Béjart, Georges Pinel, Germain Clérin, Nicolas Bonenfant (a young law clerk still articled), Madeleine Malingre, and Catherine Désurlis—in all, ten actors. Their names are rich in an archaic charm, evocative of both the boards and the guild of lawyers' clerks. These "youngsters of background" must rather have given the effect of youngsters free as air. The Illustre Théâtre was formally established on June 30, 1643 by an instrument executed before a Paris notary, one Fieffé.

As the scene of their endeavors they chose the Gardeners' Tennis Court, near the Nesle gate, just about where the Rue de Seine now meets the Rue Mazarine. The rental was 1900 livres a year for three years, payable in advance. Security was demanded for the fulfillment of the contract, and Madeleine's mother, now for some months a widow, had to pledge her real estate. The company was able to start its performances at the beginning of January 1644; it had made an experimental beginning at Rouen in the preceding November.

At first the venture achieved only a middling success. The Hôtel de Bourgogne and the Théâtre du Marais were formidable competition for unknown beginners, and there may not have been at that time enough customers to keep three theaters flourishing, of which the most recent was not far removed from an amateur enterprise. Nevertheless the new company fought to maintain itself. In June it signed a dancer named Mallet. The contract, dated June 28, was signed "Molière." Jean Baptiste had adopted the name that stands for his undying glory. He had succeeded Denys Bey as manager and responsible business director of the troupe. It had not taken him long to accomplish it.

Collapse ensued with no great delay. Its causes seem fairly obvious. An insufficiency of original capital and the costs incurred in order to make a showing soon forced the new troupe into contracting debts. In order to discharge these—as a prelude to the prompt contraction of fresh ones—the company put itself at the mercy of a moneylender named Pommier, and in his own interest he took a lien on the Illustre Théâtre's future profits—imaginary profits. When the receipts obstinately refused to increase, the site was blamed for it. The company moved, and at the beginning of 1645 we find it settled in the Black Cross Tennis Court—Jeu de Paume de la Croix-Noire—on the Quai des Ormes, now the Quai des Célestins. But proximity to the Théâtre du Marais did not improve its lot. There were now only eight players: Molière, Bey, Pinel, Clérin, Madeleine and Geneviève Béjart, Madeleine Malingre, and Catherine Bourgeois. The ones recently recruited had fled the storm about to break. Molière, debt-ridden, was compelled to offer his creditors unsalable pledges. Shut up in the Châtelet on the application of his chandler, to whom he owed 142 livres, he found himself being supported by Pommier the moneylender, who had met all costs, including that of the transfer to the Black Cross, and without seeing anything coming in. A friendly police court judge arranged matters, but Pommier reasserted his claim. Then a pavior, Léonard Aubry, stood security for the debtor. Molière, at the last glimpse we have of him in this year of distress, is still in debtors' prison, put there at the instance of his linen draper.

Such in brief is the story of the Illustre Théâtre. It is the story of many a new enterprise, and Molière's debts look trivial compared with those of the young Balzac. Not that he lacked support. He had it to begin with from Béjart's widow, who was always ready to guarantee anything she was asked to, even to hypothecating houses that were already mortgaged, and who vouched for Molière quite as for her own children. He had it from Tristan L'Hermite, who worked his exalted connections and got permission for the Illustre Théâtre to put itself under the patronage of His Royal Highness the Duc d'Orléans. He had it from the plays he put on, particularly Du Ryer's *Scévole*, Tristan's own *Malheurs Domestiques du Grand Constantin* and *La Mort de Sénèque*, and de Magnon's *Artaxerce*—all of them tragedies in the flamboyant manner of the time and perfect indices of the actors' preferences. The Illustre Théâtre's setback, I think, taught Molière a lesson and taught it even more effectively to Madeleine. Both were as different as could be from Balzac in business matters; both were methodical and anxious to combine prestige with profits.

It is not known whether Molière had to listen to his father's "I told you so." Monsieur Poquelin conducted himself as a fair-minded parent and a man solicitous of his family's good name, even when the name was masked under a pseudonym. He indemnified Léonard Aubry and squared Molière's other obligations. When we remember that he had spent a good deal of money on his son's education and that the son had requited him by going on the stage in association with socially negligible and morally dubious persons, we can but admire the paternal behavior. Michaut shows conclusively that the relationship of the two was, from first to last, bland, reasonable, and characterized by a seemly restraint. Later on, Molière, become wealthy, made his father an important loan in the name of his friend Rohault in order to forestall any contest of his father's will by the family.

So much for the early shaping of Molière and for his point of departure, so far as they are to be descried through extremely reticent documents and all manner of biographical fabrications. A sound education; the influences of open-minded and freethinking intimates; immersion in the Béjart environment, in which middle-class values underwent constant attrition; the persistence of middle-class propensities whether or no; a vocational urge that was evidently irresistible— these we can make out, but hardly the man himself. Molière was far from being one of those geniuses who attain their full stature at a bound. What he needed was time and the inexorable pressure of experience.

CHAPTER TWO

APPRENTICESHIP

While the actors chattered briskly about their concerns, Wilhelm remained lost in thought.

GOETHE

I

THE PARIS venture and its failure can hardly be reckoned as part of Molière's apprenticeship. Rather it was a first tentative start toward a goal—a start that arrived nowhere, but still had value as a test, like the first serious spills of one who will yet be an accomplished horseman. Almost immediately, in 1646, we discover Molière in the provinces, more absorbed in his calling than ever, graduating rather rapidly from nameless obscurity to a featured eminence, and then making his company and his methods felt with all that technical mastery that was doubtless his most amazing attribute.

At the thought of Molière in the provinces a hundred picaresque impressions swarm to the mind's eye. We think of belated arrivals at shabby inns, robberies, set-tos in forest glades, bedraggled costumes, picturesque makeshifts, squabbles between actors, slaps, dodges, tatters. We know now that so far as Molière is concerned these impressions are baseless. He made his start, along with the Béjarts, in a company already established and pretty well equipped—that of Dufresne, who benefited by the favor of the governor of Guyenne, Louis de Nogaret, Duc d'Épernon. Later, but not much later, Molière's own company was gathering compliments on "the lavishness of the costumes." Anyway, the picaresque aspects of these tours —save for the fresh and vitalizing wind that streams from them through his works—were pretty certainly not what captured his interest; and what captured his interest should capture ours as we think about him.

The picaresque way of life, if compulsory, is a starveling's; if voluntary, a daydreamer's or an anarchist's. Molière was poor only by a trick of fate; and if by chance he daydreamed—indeed, what else was one to do through those long hours on the road?—his daydreams were soon to unite, coalesce, and shape themselves and to count toward the enrichment of a stock of creative power that was likewise a stock in trade. Between the course pursued by a Molière, all progress and practicality, and the aimless drifting of the *picaro* there is a difference in kind that our fondness for what is picturesque ought not to make us overlook. We come on various passages of Molière's life at which it may be admissible to speak of pathos, but these tours are not among them—unless indeed we elect to call everything pathetic that we have never coped with ourselves.

We must bear in mind, too, that barnstorming the provinces in that period was no longer an adventure and nothing else. It involved the exciting possibility that an adventure of sorts might turn into a business success. By a royal decree of April 16, 1641 it was forbidden to treat stage folk as bemeaned by their profession or to make them the victims of public social discrimination. To be sure, the general prejudice persisted, especially in the middle class; but the upshot was recognition of theater folk as counting socially. Molière, for example, did not lose anything of his status as an official of the royal household or of his middle-class connections. The craze for the theater was such that many a member of the provincial aristocracy appeared under the stage candelabra or even as manager of a troupe; witness that Sieur de Monchaigre, seigneur of La Brosse in Anjou, after whom Scarron modeled a character in *Le Roman Comique*. The theater of that time may be likened to a branch of trade long crippled by overburdensome legal restrictions and then suddenly relieved of them. Enterprising persons saw a chance to make hay. Madeleine Béjart and Molière were apparently among the enterprising. We surmise that they were methodical, at once patient and energetic, with a longing eye turned Parisward at the smallest hint of opportunity; susceptible to weariness, no doubt, but no less so to anything that promised a deliberate progress secure against reversals.

At that particular juncture touring the provinces was a tactical necessity. Molière had experienced, if but indirectly, the effects of the Hôtel de Bourgogne's overwhelming monopoly. He saw the provinces less as a training ground than as a huge employment office. In them were to be found princely patrons. The governor of Guyenne or of Languedoc was closer to the royal court than the Parisian populace was. Acting folk, so far from letting the prevailing wind blow them whithersoever it listed, sought it out —whence a certain amount of preliminary wasted motion as they cast about for some grandee enamored of the stage. This waste of motion seems to have been spared Molière. The Duc d'Épernon, who was a good deal of a pain to his people in Guyenne and was trying to be a pleasure to his mistress, the beautiful Ninon de Lartiges, had become the patron of Dufresne's troupe, and Molière contrived to make the most of the opportunity. The company, as we have seen, had a very respectable standing; indeed, it ranked as a model of its kind, and Destin, the hero of Scarron's *Roman Comique*, speaks of it with deference. Molière is not at first in evidence: it is Dufresne who is in the Duc's good graces, and anyway a debt-ridden man does not pine to strew his name right and left on the applications and other papers that actors are perpetually executing. But we shall not see him continuing long in obscurity. It is not very probable that he acted in Bordeaux, but Cadillac, the Duc's château, must have supplied him with a makeshift stage, as practically any château of the period would have done. People satisfied their insistent appetite for the theater as best they could. They picked out the biggest place available; if they had a guardroom, so much the better, and if they must make shift with a bed-chamber, so much the worse. The actors could count on hangings—they were plentiful everywhere—and on some boxes of candles and some seats that would be all but intermingled with those occupied by the persons of quality who made up the audience. They could not count on either acting room or expressive scenery. They had to underline effects, individualize themselves by speech and facial expression, and create the illusion of remoteness by the magic of suggestion.

Molière and the Béjarts followed the itinerary of the company and of its patron, whose troubles with the Guyenne population were going from bad to worse. In 1646 the plague invaded Bordeaux, and the Duc d'Épernon was in Paris. In 1647 Dufresne's company was, or is supposed to have been, at Toulouse, Albi, and Carcassonne. In 1648 the people of Bordeaux rebelled outright against their governor—an event that appears to have brought about a serious displacement of the company's center of gravity. On April 23, 1648 the city corporation of Nantes gave an audience to one "Morlierre," who was there to request permission for himself and his associates to take over the theater for performances of their repertoire. His reception was rather chill. His Honor Marshal de la Meilleraye was ill, and the actors were requested to await his recovery. The wait dragged on until May 17; then the license was at last issued. History, or at any rate tradition, informs us that the troupe had only a middling success. One Segale, a Venetian, is supposed to have hurt it by the popularity of his puppet show and his mechanical contrivances.

In this transaction in which the name "Molière" turns up for the first time, albeit in a twisted version, two details may well claim our attention. The first is that we find Molière appearing by himself and pre-ferring a petition in advance of the company's arrival. He is already Comedy's mouthpiece, guide, and en-voy. In that capacity we shall perceive him almost invariably henceforth, quick to come forward, to unsnarl complications, and to take upon himself the burden imposed by others' distrust and obstructiveness; a discreet helmsman, a resourceful and spirited negotiator who undoubtedly perceives in every invitation to let down his guard an invitation to make himself felt. Such a man we surmise that he was at Nantes; such a man we shall find him in the assembly hall of the Petit Louvre, confronting the king; and as such a man we shall give him our admiration in his *Impromptu* and in his *Critique de l'École des Femmes*. Among the typical pictures of Molière that we conjure up, one seems to me to stand out pre-eminently: the picture of a Molière bowing from the waist, right foot forward, leg slightly bent at the knee, hat in hand, wig pendent, speech unhurried and responsive to the play of mood on the face of the one besought.

And the second striking detail, whether fact or legend, is the grim competition with the exhibitor of mechanical contrivances. We find a man of Venice at the outset and a man of Florence at the close of this career whose profounder meanings were consistently subordinated to the wayward principles of entertainment. Lully was ultimately to persuade Molière of what Segale had contrived to foreshadow: to wit, the deep-seated contradiction inherent in the attendant circumstances governing the expression of his genius. We shall see, furthermore, that Molière was not the man to make an issue of a contradiction or two.

We shall make no attempt to retrace step by step the details of his comings and goings, which are imperfectly known anyway. He is supposed to have been hissed in Limoges on account of Pourceaugnac; but that is mere assumption. There is one other invention that we find more beguiling. There was living near Angoulême a woman named Escars, a descendant of the family that was visiting Montaigne after his return from Italy. This woman had married a Comte de Baignac. "Escar-Baignac" easily becomes, in a play, "Escarbagnac." Suffer the names of Montaigne and Molière to be thus linked, that the two may be kins-

men in the realm of anecdote as they are in that of
reasoning.

With the year 1649 our actors resume the south-
eastward course that would soon become their regular
itinerary. It is interesting to learn that Dufresne was
summoned to Agen by order of the governor and
that the city authorities had a theater built for him
in a tennis court. The troupe was likewise recruited
for the festival at Toulouse, where the city magistrates
appropriated seventy-five livres for a performance to
celebrate the arrival of the Comte du Roure, the
king's lieutenant general.

On January 10, 1650, at Narbonne, Molière stood
godfather to a child born out of wedlock. Until recent
times there could still be seen in Narbonne the Hôtel
des Trois Nourrices, a perfect specimen of the inns at
which Molière alighted. A former residence dating
from 1528, it stood in the vicinity of one of the city
gates. The outer walls were pierced by huge cross-
barred windows with mullions richly sculptured. The
window on the southern façade bore on its two up-
rights, on the center mullion, and on the frame the
busts of huge-breasted women. Let us imagine, if you
will, the troupe's arrival here at nightfall. Let it be a
January nightfall of this Mediterranean region, so still
that the blandness of the air seems an emanation of
the very stillness. Children, men, and women gather
around in the dust, with a babel of chatter in unintel-
ligible Southland dialect, and watch the unloading of
great trunks stuffed with mysteries, out of which peep
here and there, where they were imperfectly closed,
bits of gold or silver embroidery, velvet, and jewels
as disturbing as if they were genuine. Madeleine Béjart, her mind on the list of properties, is calm of eye
and steadily smiling. Dufresne arranges for rooms,
amid outcries of servants and the innkeeper's voluble
assurances. Molière dismounts from his horse and goes
to find an easy chair to drop into. He is drawing
together the threads of a scene thought up on the
road, or he is thinking ahead to the next stand, or

he is simply relaxing, although it is still second nature to him to register the faces and the gesticulations that he can make out in the shadowy light. Upstairs there is the laughter or the bickering of the other actors, with scraps of argument re-echoing; there is the intimacy of minds, of bodies; there are the first premonitory rustlings of night. It seems probable that Molière at this stage of his career was already working with machinelike precision and that he was totally absorbed in his job—one of the most engaging in existence, and in both senses of the word if we bear in mind that the most insignificant adventures or gestures or acts could serve him as points of departure for his technical inventiveness. Obsessed by a longing for pre-eminence—for no man was ever more ambitious—he was already under pressures of space, of time. Later, in Paris, these would become overwhelming and a threat to his balance. But it is credible that in 1650, on the eve of his adventures in Lyons and of his conquest of Conti's favor, he was carrying his load lightly and tasting the delights of the man aware that he is duly ripening; tasting them with the more enjoyment because his success was still far short of brilliant enough to evoke the two worst hardships of a life of struggle, envy and the competition of equals.

When he went upstairs to his bedroom, was it to be again with his mistress of long standing, Madeleine? Very likely it was. Molière, like many a voluptuary of sorts, was a man of regular habits.

The summer of 1650 marks a turning point in Molière's career. The Duc d'Épernon, forced into relinquishing Guyenne for good and all, dropped his troupe of actors. If, about that time, Dufresne stopped managing the company, as has been presumed with some reason, it was just about then that Molière established his leadership of it. He was not to give up that leadership again until his death. This company of players was already well recognized. Molière was now becoming its undisputed head. It had taken him five years to reach that consummation. Five years is a short

enough time if we take into consideration the early
setbacks and the difficulties of getting started. Let us,
then, be not overready to deplore the trials that our
great man had to undergo. Rather, we should take
satisfaction in the earliest triumphs of one of the most
successful careers ever chronicled

II

Now occurs a momentous development. Molière's
troupe, after several tours of the coastal region of
Carcassonne and of Provence, set its course for Lyons,
which it reached sometime in the closing months of
1652. Lyons was to be its base until well into 1655.

Acting in Lyons was an altogether different affair
from acting in one or another provincial small town.
The Lyons public had attained in matters theatrical a
degree of independence of Paris. Despite the continuing obstructiveness of the aldermen, private middle-
class initiative and the provincial governors' sympathy
had prepared the public for shrewd and exacting appraisal of dramatic affairs. In 1538 a wealthy merchant, Jean Neyron, had inaugurated at his own expense an auditorium for theatrical performances in
the Rue des Bouchers. The printers' guild, which then
set the pitch of middle-class society as the personages
of the silk industry do today, co-operated valiantly.
Lyons was a city that baffled the understanding of
Parisians, and its appetite for pleasure and luxury was
combined, we are told, with "an excessive addiction
to humility"; but Molière was to find here a state of
affairs quite unlike the savage competition of one
company with another. He was to find something that
was and still is, outside Paris, a rarity in the domain
of the arts: a tradition richly instructive on the technical side.

Lyons was a gateway of France that stood wide
open to Italy, and the Italians had brought the theater
to a phase of maturity and merit unknown in France.
Lyons had welcomed Italian actors ahead of Paris:
as early as 1513 it had licensed the erection of acting

platforms by Florentine actors at the Porcherie Well. At the time when Molière established himself in the city, people still remembered the funeral observances for Isabella Andreini, star of the historic company known as the Gelosi—They Who Bring Pleasure; she had died in 1604 after a miscarriage, while on her way from Paris to Italy, laden with distinctions conferred by the French queen. Public tribute was paid her, and in her funeral procession were mace-bearers carrying the municipal colors, and behind them the merchant guilds bearing torches. It was a funeral that, seen in retrospect, makes an ironic contrast with Molière's. Isabella Andreini had been as beautiful as she was good ("Casto conjugio, sophia, vultusque decore"). She had been a member of a number of academies, among them the Intenti of Pavia, in which the name she bore was "L'Accesa"—She of the Loving Heart. Tasso had inscribed verses to her, and in a Roman festival arranged by Cardinal Aldobrandini her picture had been placed between Tasso's and Petrarch's. She had composed plays; also a pastoral poem already seven times reprinted. To reconstitute an Isabella Andreini for our latter day would require an amalgamation in one person of Sarah Bernhardt and Madame de Noailles. The Gelosi, renowned in their day, included players to be ranked as true literati. Their example and the memory of them could not but strengthen the middle-class actor and literatus that Molière was.

The Italians, including the Gelosi themselves, were not merely finished and cultivated artists. The *commedia dell' arte* of the time was a far cry from the moonlit world of Watteau. With its extraordinary motley of multicolored gesticulating mountebanks, their faces hidden under stiff leather masks with matted manes, its zanies, its Harlequins in attitudes that perpetually mocked the laws of gravity, its swashbucklers roaring out *concetti*, its insinuating, lewd, scented hussies, its jumble of bodies and of shrieks, this species of comedy, by dint of its expert but coarse acrobatics, its *lazzi* punctuated with quoted scraps of Seneca and Montaigne, released in the people the whole complex explosive power of the Renaissance. An entertainment for the populace that was to the advantage of the upper classes, a form of social realism that proliferated social types as the motion picture does now, it wrought its lasting though bloodless revolution under the stage lights and rent society from bottom to top. In a period dominated by Platonism, nothing was more anti-Platonic than the *commedia dell' arte*. It signified, not the dethronement of ideas, but a thrust delivered from below against the whole cosmos of ideas—a sort of philosophical peasant uprising at sound of Punchinello's whistle and the thwacks of Harlequin's wooden sword. But the *commedia*, while it is unadulterated action, is critical action, since its action is comic. By carrying its anti-Platonism to the logical extreme it creates typical figures that, while standing for a multitude of individuals, have lives of their own not traceable to any particular individual. Harlequin, an African slave to begin with, was not this or that African slave; Pedrolino may have been a peasant, but Pierrot's lineage is lost in the obscurity of ages. The precise moment when the individual became generalized eludes definition. The types found in the *commedia dell' arte* come to us, by virtue of mask and costume and standardized gesture, endowed with personalities at once representative and specific, greatly resembling those of the animals of fable. Among these types and the successive players who depict them the give-and-take has endless variety. They are types that evolve in the same way as the sentiments that in the course of centuries will cluster in all their transmogrifications around a single personage. If it be true that the dramatic poet needs to base his creations on such anonymous folk creations, the *commedia dell' arte* can account in large measure for the wonderful distinctness of Molière's creations. It is thanks to the *commedia* that seventeenth-century comedy had ready to hand

a usable mythology; not at all a literary one such as
that of tragedy, but a living and a real one—as real as
was ever the mythology of Olympus to an early
Greek.

Beyond question Molière profited substantially by
what the *commedia* had to teach. His earliest plays
draw their inspiration from the Italian patterns. Traces
of them are omnipresent in Lyons. Later on, in Paris,
his company had to alternate with an Italian troupe,
and at that time he was free for intensive study of
the most celebrated mimes from across the Alps.
Scaramouche, who, holding the future Louis XIV in
his arms, made the little dauphin laugh so hard he
forgot that he was housebroken, Scaramouche who
was nature's pupil and Molière's schoolmaster, must
powerfully have affected the creator of Monsieur
Jourdain. And since at this point we are within the
orbit in which the Italian influence is the most pronounced, this is the place to say that Molière seems
to have salvaged from the *commedia dell' arte* whatever was consonant with his own innate genius.

It would appear, punditical opinion to the contrary
notwithstanding, that one of Molière's cardinal
achievements was the rescue of the drama from literature, or, more precisely, the rescue of dramatic
literature from literature. Whatever interpretation of
this dictum is necessary boils down to the following:

In the *commedia dell' arte* the literary constituent
—the spoken word, the sentence—is made secondary
to the other constituents, as the body's motions, the
mimetic gestures. The spoken word occurs as something inserted in a rhythmic design akin to that of
gymnastics or of the dance. Reading the script of a
commedia al improviso would no more take the place
of seeing the performance than reading a motion
picture script would. Furthermore—and here we have
the inmost significance of the improvisatory rationale
—histrionic invention takes place *on the stage;* it is
dictated by the available acting room, the personalities
and capacities of the actors, the effects produced by

their coming face to face on the boards. Regardless
of the innumerable modifications that the spirit of the
commedia was then undergoing, its spirit always enjoined that dramatic ideas should find rhythmical
expression by means of nonliterary utterances; that
each should flower out of the preceding one as the
figures of a dance do, or the movements of a gymnastic routine. It will be pointed out that the drama
according to Molière is a drama of written words—
one that can be resurrected practically *in toto* by the
process of reading. But that demur leaves us facing
this consideration: Molière found the way to devise
a speech that should precisely mirror the body's motions and the rhythmic comings and goings within
the area of the stage. No one need hear very many
performances of his plays to discover how closely the
dialogue (with, likewise, the structure of the scenes)
resembles dance figures, and even more closely the
figures of calisthenics; how tightly the verbal interchanges are linked together by purely physical thrust
and parry; how uniformly the extraordinary emphasis
of these interchanges comes not so much from their
own expressiveness as from a sort of muscular explosion that projects them as from a catapult. We
shall see that Molière's genius consisted in superposing
the mental effect and the physical—of making dance
and demonstration one. Scaramouche, we are told,
spoke but little and expressed himself with difficulty;
but he conveyed his meanings to perfection by grimaces and postures. Molière succeeded in creating a
literary idiom of grimaces and postures. The Italian
comic actors, using their highly specialized and precise
technique, provided him with a simplified and, as it
were, a pristine working model of this signal accomplishment.

Furthermore, it was in connection with acrobatic
prowess that Molière apparently achieved his most
intimate acquaintanceship with the folk of the Italian
theater. In the Lyons of that period a very fetching
carnival actress was displaying herself in the interest

of an Italian hawker named Jacomo de Gorla, her putative father. This Marquise-Thérèse de Gorla exploited her litheness on a platform lengthened by an optical illusion. "She executed some remarkable acrobatics," a contemporary reports. "Her legs and part of her thighs were visible, because her skirt was slit at either side, and her hose were modestly fastened at the top to short underpants." This "Marquise," whose ostensible first name would inevitably produce on snobs of a later day the opposite effect to that intended, was destined to wreak havoc on the susceptibilities of our great men, for, if we must trust the record, those who one after another fell in love with her were Molière, both Corneilles, La Fontaine, and Racine. We know the lofty and artless lines that Pierre Corneille later addressed to her. A "graybeard such as he" would probably not have been in the way of observing her, as Molière did, so frivolously costumed in those rudimentary tights, with "her hose modestly fastened at the top to short underpants." And, just as probably, Molière, who had come upon her on the mountebank's platform, among the dust and impudicities of the public square, doing handstands in front of the chest of nostrums that her father was hawking, would never have been able to take with her the tone that came so naturally to the author of *Cinna*. What is so appealing about Molière is that he picks up life by its commonplace everyday handle, without being suffered to retain for any length of time the illusions that come to him about others. Unquestionably charged with ardor and with ideal aspirations—with a degree of illusion, too, if you like—he is forbidden every sort of posturing, even the nobleminded sort. His very profession put him on the unfinished side of the scenery. It followed that his sentiments were conspicuously unliterary, and that in an age when sentiments were literary *in excelsis*.

This encounter of Molière's company with the Italians paved the way to an illustrious career for Marquise de Gorla. In February 1653 she married

René Berthelot, known as du Parc or Gros-René, one of the company's better actors; and so she acquired the name under which she became famous. In Molière's being enamored of a young woman simultaneously with her marriage to one of his associates there is nothing that need astonish us. A mixed-up code of morals easily takes charge in circles in which impulses are not inhibited by middle-class requirements. Is not Molière credited about the same time with a liaison with Mademoiselle de Brie?—to say nothing at this point about the mystery of Armande, to which we shall duly come. Biographers make hard work of admitting these facts; the better ones try to forgive Molière. He is neither forgivable nor a subject for forgiveness. He was a sensualist, and his tubercular tendency may have heightened his sensuality—a sensualist surrounded by alluring women, exposed to all a stage manager's temptations and possessed of all the carnal appetites of a man both intense and wearied. A life cannot be disordered except as it has had some order that is disrupted. In this department Molière was living his life at the instinctive level, with no sense of degradation and no actual degradation. Assuredly we can distinguish a moral order in his plays; but that order is really an outgrowth of his works, shaped out of the raw experience of life. And that is beyond our appraisal.

In 1653—according to some authorities, 1655—L'Étourdi was acted at Lyons. With this play we emerge from the stage of apprenticeship, at least so far as the quality of the work is concerned, though it is conventional to extend Molière's apprenticeship as far as his establishment in Paris. In L'Étourdi he first shows himself master of a diction original in flavor, of an irresistible pace and spiritedness. Not that we can altogether share the enthusiasm of Victor Hugo, who reconstituted the seventeenth century to suit himself. The animation of the play is not so much the animation of comedy as an experiment in pure diversion, in buffoonery. In it youthful mettle displaces critical insight. The theme, being extraneous to the sentiments expressed and yet in control of them, makes game of them according to the exigencies of the plot. Molière gives evidence of his ability to create persons who are alive, but he has not yet attained the level of creating thought that is alive. He does not even seem to be so alert as he later becomes about pre-empting the best thoughts already in circulation. In *Il Inavvertito*, the play by the comedian Beltrame that Molière took as his source, there is a delightful device not to be found in *L'Étourdi*. At the end Fulvio (of whom Lélie is the counterpart) does not dare consummate his happiness for fear of committing some fresh stupidity, and with his eyes he silently begs Scapin to come to the rescue. This is an effect of no little drollery, in which the character neatly doubles back on himself—no doubt the one purely comic touch in the whole play. On the other hand the dialogue in *L'Étourdi*, though less familiar and less racy than that of *Il Inavvertito*, is brisker and more casual; it foreshadows thus early Molière's happiest vein. The sprightly, piquant Mascarille has ceased to be the acrobatic valet of the Italians; he has a pride of his own, his own little inner world of affectations; the mountebank in him is merged with the lower-middle-class citizen. And the spoken interchanges are already calling one another forth with the elastic elegance that would presently put Molière's comic dialogue in a class by itself. In a list of plays that includes *Le Menteur*, *L'Étourdi* is hardly to be ranked as anything apocalyptic or revolutionary; but it is a decidedly striking anticipation, especially for us who know what it anticipates.

III

A benefit performance for charity by Molière's company on February 9, 1653 brought in 308 livres —good takings for the period; good takings for the provinces, we might add, had the place been other than Lyons.

That first season in Lyons established Molière's
company and left it well grounded in self-confidence.
Its reputation and its resources were already considerable, as is shown by the imposing developments that
now awaited it in Languedoc. For it made sallies in
all directions from Lyons, but chiefly southward; and
it was in the south about the beginning of autumn in
1653.

It was then just a year since the young king of
France had come back into his capital city amid ac-
clamations of adherents of the Fronde, now sickened
of their unavailing commotions. The prodigal nobles
had come to terms with Mazarin; his supreme power,
now regained and solidified, was soon to usher in that
of Louis XIV himself. Among the amnesties granted
was one to Armand de Bourbon, Prince de Conti,
who for three consecutive years was to preside over
the Languedoc Estates in the king's name. This prince,
insignificant and as if in eclipse between his brother
the great Condé and his adored sister Madame de
Longueville, undersized, warped, and freakish, witty
by turns in the trivial sense of the word and in its
exalted sense, was thoroughly typical of the Frondeurs of royal lineage, and for the reason that he was
something of a caricature of them. Those princes
were the victims of a disastrous incohesiveness,
chargeable even less to their omnivorous novel-reading
than to the discrepancy between their power to do
things and the utter inanity of what they did. Not
being as yet in the presence of a visible source of
completely unmistakable and completely acknowledged power, they lived surrounded by the possible,
the attainable. Whatever they willed was *ipso facto*
practicable; but what they thought they were willing,
they were only imagining. Drawing the line between
the will and the imagination was to be the task of the
century's second half, and particularly the task of
Molière. Those princes saw things on a grandiose
scale, and they took themselves the way they saw
other things. When Mademoiselle de Montpensier

fired on Turenne's troops from the Bastille it never occurred to her to assimilate the deed to a considered and serious policy: the deed flashed upon her by itself, in all its magnificent isolation, as owing its meaning not at all to its own purport, but to its being performed by her. The fashionable romanticism clothed this delusion of power in glowing colors. The blue sashes, violins, and trumpets that Retz mentions are straight out of *Astrée*. We sense the delightful and intoxicating atmosphere of this infatuated epoch—the imperceptible glide from reading into acting, the memories of daydreams getting mixed up with perceptions of reality, the masked ball that overflows into the street, its mimic impersonations already a part of history. Those Danaides of power consume themselves so senselessly, smashing their country as if it were a plaything, that we become incensed with them, and we get to the point of holding it against Corneille that he exalts without castigating them. Nevertheless this masquerade was of considerable profit to clear-sighted spectators of the frolic. It taught them or reminded them that neither will nor power is of avail for those who despise the prosaic terms of reality; that effective power is the outcome of an exceedingly delicate balance of forces that fantasy never attains. The cumbrous royal engine—which itself was to be derailed in a time not too remote—was then teaching that very lesson of prose and moderation. We may presume without much fear of self-deception that Molière had, in the Prince de Conti, an excellent visible object lesson in the selfsame delusion of power that he was to condemn as long as he lived.

Armand de Bourbon had originally intended himself for the Church. It is related that one day, seeing a fine body of troops drawn up in an open space, he was smitten by the notion of being a general. Bishop turns into general simply by a dictate of his own impulses. On the same system the general can turn into a monarch; that is, become a conspirator. Conti was doubtless sick of amusing himself and plying his intrigues while overshadowed by his portentous family. And then his cause was defeated. Mazarin was perfectly content to cultivate pleasant relations with the Prince. As a matter of fact, there was one of his seven nieces, the virtuous Anne Martinozzi, whom he had to get settled in life. We come, then, to the juncture at which Conti, at La Grange, his château near Pézenas in Bas-Languedoc, was negotiating his marriage agreement. His secretary, the poet and schemer Sarrazin, had obtained permission for the Prince's mistress, Madame de Calvimont, to live with him. Another member of the Prince's household staff, Abbé de Cosnac, the future Archbishop of Aix, discovered that Molière's company was in the vicinity. Conti doted on comedy, and Cosnac took it upon himself to summon the troupe to La Grange. Meanwhile there came to Pézenas another troupe managed by one Cormier, an old-time Pont Neuf practitioner and past master of all the tricks of the trade. Cormier took to showering presents on Madame de Calvimont. The lady's influence was still considerable, and it was Cormier's troupe that was engaged. When Abbé de Cosnac told the Prince about his commitment with Molière, Conti merely commented that it was more fitting for his representative to break his promise than for himself to break his.

"Molière turned up, however," Cosnac recorded, "and when he asked that he be paid at least the amount of the expense he had been put to in coming, I was unable to get it for him, although the claim was largely just. Monsieur the Prince de Conti had seen fit to be obstinate about this trifle. This sorry behavior vexed me, and I determined to have the company act in the Pézenas theater and to give them a thousand écus myself, rather than not keep my word.

"When they were ready to act in the town Monsieur the Prince de Conti, a little injured in his dignity by what I had done, and coaxed by Sarrazin, whom I had got disposed to be of help to me, assented to their coming to put on one performance in the theater at

La Grange. The company in its first performance failed to please Madame de Calvimont and hence to please Monsieur the Prince de Conti, although in the opinion of all the rest of the audience it was immeasurably better than Cormier's troupe, alike in the excellence of the performance and the handsomeness of the costumes. A few days later they performed again, and Sarrazin, by dint of singing their praises, made Monsieur the Prince de Conti admit that Molière's troupe must be engaged and Cormier's dismissed. He, Sarrazin, had at first taken their side at my instance, but presently, having fallen in love with du Parc, he was serving his own purposes. He won over Madame de Calvimont, and not only did he get Cormier's troupe turned away, but he also got Molière's troupe given an allowance."

Molière and his associates were actually awarded an allowance by the Prince, and they renamed themselves "The Actors of Monsieur the Prince de Conti's Company"—no mean achievement for one throw of the dice. I hardly understand how Sainte-Beuve can be disturbed by the thought that this signal triumph of Molière hinged on Madame de Calvimont's self-interest and Sarrazin's hankering for a pretty circus girl. Was not that sort of thing an integral circumstance of the profession? And was it not a good thing that Molière should get some experience of that kind of training before he tackled Paris? Why should anyone want to fence off a man's genius from the practical requirements of the calling in which his genius was made manifest? And if anyone chooses to emphasize a wry incompatibility between such obligations and the purity of the genius, let him reflect that the genius is brought into being by the very incompatibility that he deplores. But for those exacerbations, those vexatious obstacles, we should almost certainly never have had the nimble-witted, burdened, penetrating Molière we know. Give a thought, too, to what Cosnac's invitation meant to him. It was an extremely lucky conjuncture that might provide him—as it actually did—with a patron of high degree who stood well at court, one by whose help he might get back into Paris earlier and under better auspices. When Molière went to Pézenas he saw his imaginable success there as far transcending the details of its achievement, whatever they might be. How poignant, then, his disappointment on listening to Cosnac's embarrassed explanation! In his capacity as a good employer he demanded at least reimbursement for the company's traveling expenses; but when he realized the Abbé's benevolence he calmed down, and we conceive him as amenable to any directions given him. If it is easy for us to imagine his satisfaction on learning of Sarrazin's co-operativeness, we can guess his feelings when he discovered that Conti's secretary had a private reason for standing by him. Conceivably his pleasure contained an admixture of jealousy. We think we can descry in Molière—as clearly as is possible from so far and without personal documents— both a private life subject to all the ups-and-downs of emotion and mood, and a kind of professional sensitivity that made him exploit his woes and his enjoyments promptly and cleverly for the sake of a definite, attainable end. Start with the notion of *getting ahead*, in every sense that the phrase includes; elevate it into an instinctive drive, an actuating condition; and you will arrive at what was Molière's powerful and steady motive force. Now, in this Pézenas affair we see him getting ahead, forcing his way, conquering new territory and new repute. If his company was truly the better of the two, if it won its place for good and with great rapidity, you may be sure that it was not solely because Sarrazin lusted after du Parc. Conti's relish for comedy was one trump card in the deck. Up to the time when the Prince miserably trampled on the very thing that had meant so much to him Molière appears to have stayed in his good graces— indeed, so securely that on Sarrazin's death the following year a report gained currency that Conti offered Molière the unfilled position of private secretary.

Inasmuch as the Prince de Conti was for that year and the two following years president of the Estates of Languedoc, which were responsible for the appropriation of funds for the royal treasury, Molière's troupe had a quasi-official assignment to keep these gentlemen entertained. The following year we come upon the company once more, this time at Montpellier, where the Estates were now in session. Conti was returning from a victorious campaign in Catalonia. He had played the general very successfully, but he had been less lucky in love: he had caught what biographers are given to calling "a shameful disease" —a mischance entailing all manner of embarrassments, for he had now been for some months Anne Martinozzi's husband. Only two bedrooms were bespoken for him at Montpellier—two bedrooms "that would serve the purpose if carpeted with Bergama rugs and supplied with two or three cot beds to accommodate a few officers." But anyway there had to be two bedrooms. The Princess was not to submit for very long to this enforced continence. Indeed, Mazarin was writing to Colbert: "You may speak of the matter again to Madame la Princesse and say to her that she will not suffer it for long if her husband is constantly with her." The diversion of drama must have been a godsend to the one-time Frondeur, now reduced to a factitious self-restraint, and to his young wife, whose virtue had entitled her to a better lot.

At the 1655 carnival Molière's troupe regaled the princely pair with the *Ballet des Incompatibles*. Conformably to usage, several nobles who were lovers of the dance took part among the actors. The stage was occupied by the singing and dancing figures of various "incompatibles"—Dotard and Soldiers, Wealth and Virtue, Courtiers and Truth. One would scarcely bother to mention this divertissement—of which nothing has come down to us except its doggerel verse —were it not for its bearing a title that deserves to be applied to Molière's works collectively. What, pray, are Arnolphe and Agnès, Tartuffe and Elmire,

Alceste and Célimène, if not Incompatibles? More searchingly, we may put it that a character in Molière is comic for no reason but that he undertakes to merge attributes that are mutually contradictory, as domineeringness and love. To express an undertaking of that sort it is necessary to bring incompatibles together in one personality—to force them together. The union will not last long, because they struggle to be quit of each other in obedience to the laws of their being. And, to be even more probing, is not comedy the exposure of a basic incompatibility between what a person wants and what he is capable of?—whereas if both the will and the capability are inherent in the person, is it not on the cards that they will learn, by some hook or crook, to remain harmoniously together? Every comic scene is a Ballet of Incompatibles.

The Actors of Monsieur the Prince de Conti's Company got back to Lyons at intervals, before or after their Languedoc itinerary. In Lyons, which continued to be their second base of operations, they were joined at the beginning of July 1655 by an odd specimen who must be briefly sketched, if only because he makes so engaging a contrast with Molière.

Charles Coypeau d'Assouci, emperor of burlesque, was nearing fifty. He was still nicknamed Phoebus Wardrobin, for the reason that he kept an array of his lutes in the king's wardrobe. He composed music and verses, and inasmuch as, on the word of Boileau himself, he "found readers," he had achieved a degree of repute, though his way of life was more famous than his songs. Bohemian, jolly, slovenly, soft-hearted, he gave people what they wanted, as the saying was at that time. In that year, 1655, he was betaking himself in a vague way to Italy. He had left Paris with a curious and fetching outfit. A donkey laden with a trunk as full as it could hold of songs, sonnets, and epigrams, decked out with theorbos, and practically hidden under standard lutes, was followed by two very young musical page boys in grape pickers' jackets edged with a narrow braid of sham silver coins. Alas, any coins in evidence in an outfit of d'Assouci's could only be sham. He got his compensation by enjoying, with a simple fervor that brings back the sixteenth century or foreshadows the eighteenth, the pleasures of his vagrant journeyings by road, with thyme or heather for a bed "while by way of soothing your weariness an accommodating valet tickles the soles of your feet"; the belated arrivals at hamlets with smoking chimneys, where you made the abrupt descent toward the inn "with hardly any more need of either your feet or your legs, slipping and sliding as easily as a cask of wine that goes down into a wine cellar by itself, of its own weight." Lyons, "in comparison with Paris," impressed him as "a very fine little place." But it was a little place in which you enjoyed yourself, stayed on and on, and forgot your intended destination. "Thus," d'Assouci confides to us, "whatever hankering I might have to get across the mountains, whose whitening ridges were perpetually in sight, I could not withstand the favors that I received from all those fine people who paid every honor to my Muse and gave it every welcome. . . . But what most won me," he goes on, "was meeting Molière and the Messrs. Beiarts. Such a fascination has the drama, I could not abruptly tear myself away from those fascinating friends; and I dawdled three months in Lyons in the midst of gambling, Comedy, and banquets."

Any number of adventures came his way while he dawdled. A drunkard scuffled with him for his purse. A German tried to fleece him at rouge et noir. One of his page boys set out to drown the other in the Saône by making him think it one foot deep where it was thirty, and the unlucky miniature Pierrot had to be suspended by one foot to empty him of all the water he had swallowed. With one little merry-andrew rescued and the other page, the would-be murderer, decamped, the second one had to be replaced—though it is a trifle hard to make out whether from professional necessity or sentimental insistence on symmetry. D'Assouci heard that in Avignon there was a fine "top-register voice"—boy soprano—that would be sure to suit him perfectly. Instead, then, of following "that pleasing stream that leads to Turin," the emperor of burlesque embarked on the Rhône with Molière and his troupe. The passage was enjoyable and unadventurous. D'Assouci was down to forty pistoles, but Avignon had its Academy, "a little piece of Judea" as famous as it was awe-inspiring. "A majestic Jew named Melchizedek, long of nose and pallid of countenance, won my money, horned Moses won my ring, and Simon the Leper first won my cloak and then gave me the itch. But inasmuch as a man is never poor as long as he has friends, I, having Molière as well-wisher and the whole Beiart household as friends, in spite of the devil, fate, and all those Israelites, thought myself richer and happier than ever. For those open-handed persons did not stop at helping me as their friend: they insisted on treating me as a kinsman. Being summoned to the Estates, they took me to Pézenas with them, and I could not begin to tell all the kindnesses I received then from the whole household." They harbored him the whole winter. "Indeed, although I was in their house, I might well say that I was in my own. I never saw so much kindness, so much sincerity, or so much civility as among those people, eminently worthy as they were of actually impersonating in society the characters of the Princes whom they impersonated every day in the theater."

This account reveals the Molière of the provincial period in a very pleasing light. It reveals good nature, sincerity, generosity; the easy circumstances, not to say luxury, of these actors; an indescribable new outward and inward self-respect that both becomes them and foreshadows thus early a literary institution that is to be a credit not only to letters but also to human nature. It is a fawning recognition that d'Assouci makes—granted. But underneath the gratefulness of the coddled vagrant we detect the truth of the summary. Falling in with Molière's troupe in those days must have meant a completely refreshing discovery. The actuality should give us pause when, on the strength of entrenched legend, we are of a mind to bewail the sufferings and indignities of the itinerant great man. The vagabond in the picture is d'Assouci, not Molière, and the contrast emerges clearly enough from the pages just recapitulated. Molière's success—a sustained success that yielded speedy results and imparted to his advancement a spacious and inevitable aspect—is a challenge to us to transcend our petty sentimental weaknesses, even as Molière transcended his.

The story of his shuttlings back and forth in Languedoc is so festooned with fable that one begrudges oneself a recital of it in detail. The myths attached to a great man are fabrications made when he has become famous. His personality and bearing constitute an ideal for which no corresponding facts are discoverable. It then becomes necessary to conjure up stories, quite as in a fictional invention. The biographers that accept these tales as history commit a blunder; but the ones that discard them with contempt commit as great a blunder. They ought to cite such tales as illustratively symbolizing the inwardness of their subject. To this class of myth belongs, no doubt, that celebrated armchair in the shop of the wigmaker Gély in Pézenas, to which, it is related, Molière would go to relax and to study his fellow men. We encounter him over and over in shops in this same posture of the wordless onlooker. Frequent encounters must have given rise to such imaginary yet representative episodes. We are also shown Molière reading an illiterate girl a letter from her sweetheart, first improvising dire news, then giving her a pleasant variant, in order to make her first cry and then laugh. More plausible, if not more true, are anecdotes about the driver that trundled the actors about the region in an appalling old springless coach with unpadded seats, drawn by a crows' bait team. Sometimes in going between Pézenas and Béziers, which were about twenty-five kilometers apart, it was necessary to set out the night before. The Prince de Conti, whose requisitions cost him little, had the actors provided with horses and carriages. And to keep the refractory in hand he had the players escorted, we are told, by a troop of his company of men-at-arms.

Of the trivia that circulate about Molière we can hold to this one: that from that day to this he has been thought of as an adjuster of difficulties, a wise man of shop and highway, part comic actor and part Socrates; open-handed certainly, but also extremely clever, nimble enough to retrieve himself swiftly, and skillful at getting the laugh on his side. When he gives his expert mimicries of the Provençal traders to get a laugh out of the folk of Pézenas he knows that he is truckling to the crotchets of Languedoc. We find him likewise skillfully mimicking the Languedoc rustics for the delectation of a Provençal dinner company. What is more, he is a man that conducts his business as a shrewd tradesman. He never lets himself be overmastered in the way of a d'Assouci by the life he is living. All its components, the traveling, the quaint occurrences, the visits, the mimicries, the armchair posts of observation, are to him no more than means; and to him all these means are good.

At the beginning of November 1655 "the bishops of Béziers, Uzès, and Saint Pons, in surplices and capes, and the barons of Castries, Villeneuve, and Lanta, deputed by the Estates to felicitate His Royal Highness the Prince de Conti, betook themselves to the hostelry of Monsieur d'Alfonce, in which the said noble lord had lodgings. The Prince de Conti received them at the door of the vestibule that faces the courtyard and, having shown them in, told them that he was compelled to receive them in this place because his bedroom was all at sixes and sevens by reason of the play." Envision that bevy of nobles in full regalia; then, off at one side in the adjoining room, the complete topsyturvydom, the shifted furniture, the babel, and in the midst of it all Molière mimicking each actor in turn to encourage him in self-awareness, as he was later to do in the *Impromptu de Versailles*. All honor to this apotheosis. The patronage that Molière was enjoying was soon to end; but at least the man whom Tallemant calls "the poor little princeling" turned his back on Molière only because he was turning his back on the theater. In the Estates where the Prince had his seat the austere Pavillon was already making Jansenist approaches to him, and making them successfully. He was taking to a different game now: from soldiering and wenching he would graduate to saintliness. Actors had become repulsive, and Conti was soon talking with nothing but an odd resentment about those folk who were making an illicit use of his name. In 1662 Jean Racine was writing from Uzès: "His Lordship the Prince de Conti is three leagues from this town, and he has the province thoroughly intimidated. . . . A troupe of actors came to set up shop in a small city near here; he drove them out, and they have gone back across the Rhône. The Languedoc people are not used to this sort of reformation. Nevertheless they have to give in to it." From late 1657 Conti was complaining sourly about a particular troupe that illicitly paraded itself under his name. The troupe was Molière's. Late in life the Prince wrote a *Traité de la comédie et des spectacles selon la tradition de l'Église*, and in it the author of *Tartuffe* was represented as practically the Antichrist.

He had not yet severed relations with Molière's troupe, however, when it presented at Béziers, in December 1656, *Le Dépit Amoureux*. This play is an important milestone in Molière's progress. From a mishmash of plots, in which the few delightful passages fail to make us overlook the painfulness of the author's struggle and the tastelessness of the style, there suddenly come to bloom, as magic flowers do in fairy tales, the exquisite scenes that gave the play, with a decidedly revealing illogicality, its title. These scenes are actually no more than ancillary: yet they are the only ones acted today, so sharp is the contrast in inventiveness, in style, in poetic content—in a word, in quality—between them and the rest of the composition. The scenes of *Le Dépit Amoureux* that the theater has preserved are at the level of Molière's best. A man capable of writing them, granted the reserve fund of observation and reflection that Molière had, is ready for anything; he has mastered the whole gamut of his idiom. Éraste and Lucile have decided to part. They meet for one last time to persuade each other, and Éraste vows to Lucile—in an inexhaustible flood of eloquence—that he will never as long as he lives address another syllable to her. The charm of propinquity works on the lovers and prompts them to all manner of subterfuges for prolonging their discussion. They return each other's gifts, each other's letters, and every one of these tokens of love brings love itself back to life while ostensibly reprobating it. Presently the rupture and the quarrel have turned into a kind of veiled sadness—a new, mordant, languishing fashion of making love. Determination slides by imperceptible gradations downhill into tenderness, and when finally the word "part" is once more pronounced by Lucile, this time softly, Éraste's shock of surprise is irresistible. The part of Lucile is wonderfully contrived; it is all expectancy, all undertones, as becomes the young girl, and it is even more eloquent than the speeches of her lover.

As always in Molière at his best, this scene is rich in a variety of merits that work smoothly together—merits that can hardly be disentangled, and that it would be a shame to disentangle. Molière makes us sense from the very first, by both the comments of secondary characters and the presence of the lovers themselves, the unconquerable affinity that is to reunite Éraste and Lucile—an affinity of temperaments and of youth, a magnetism of both the senses and the mind. Molière is always able to convey to perfection that inner law of gravitation against which all our struggles are futile; but whereas in his other plays the consequences of this impotence are unsparing wounds, the defeat here is wished for and encourages the blossoming of a new happiness. In the spectator, who quickly discovers the true feelings and motives that actuate the lovers, their words create the two levels of awareness and of concern that are the essence of comic expression. But the humor here is not in the facts of the situation: it is the humor of suggestion. What I mean is that the actual fate of Éraste and Lucile is not really veiled at all, but is visible through the outward signs that seem to contradict it and are trying to contradict it, and that using the contradiction for the building-up of a suggested knowledge is pure art. The comic genius is here not satisfied to stop at mere mechanical effects: it applies its formula to the welding together of analysis and poetry. We find in *Tartuffe* and again in *Le Bourgeois Gentilhomme* some delightful echoes of this lovers' quarrel. How could Molière have forgone the repeated use of so happy a way of linking things together and of covering deficiencies? In those two plays, though, the corresponding scene lacks the elfish ease, the ethereal sensualism, that we admire in the *Dépit*—a quality that brings to mind a younger, more intense Marivaux. What some have found in this scene is a poignant emanation from Molière's own youth. I would perceive in it, rather, an expression of his maturity. It is, I must confess, not so much its artlessness as its sensualism that impresses me; and that not so much in the characters as in the author who manipulates them. I will concede that an idealized semblance of Armande might have had the power, as early as 1656, to carry Molière back to the age and the raptures of Éraste; but it is probably necessary to have got through a deal of living, and to have experienced the fading of love affairs, to appreciate the spell of a completely vernal passion in which the senses and the heart are indistinguishable, and to depict it in that idealized vein, with the gracefulness of innocence consisting in part of remorse for the loss of innocence.

The specifically theatrical side of Molière's art serves him to perfection in these scenes. In them the successive phases of emotion are staged in a way to affirm the emotions by pieces of stage business that fasten the audience's attention and give it a rhythmic pattern. Consider, for example, the pace of those opening exchanges in which Lucile's dry assents are as a stone wall from which Éraste's ranting merely rebounds; also the business of the returned gifts—passages in which the lovers' clashes obey a design as dance steps do. And the following scene, in which Marinette and Gros-René parody the reconciliation between Lucile and Éraste, is not introduced merely to relax the audience's tension and give the customers a laugh. It serves as a critical reaffirmation of what the poetic quality of the preceding scene was all but making us forget. Comic genius reclaims its prerogative, lays emphasis on the imperiousness of instinct and the futility of resistance, and reminds us that nature and reason have nothing to do with social classes. And poetic quality reasserts its prerogative in turn by means of the minor characters' diction, which uses the vernacular with a purity and a graceful correctness then unfamiliar on the stage.

This play is the high point of Molière's apprenticeship. Perhaps from that very time, and certainly within a short interval afterward, he was paving the way for his return to Paris. For that matter, he was finding Languedoc no longer auspicious. The company had passed out free admissions to *Le Dépit Amoureux* on a lavish scale. These the deputies of the assembly declined with some asperity. "As a result of the complaints put before the Estates by a number of deputies of the assembly, that the company of actors now at Béziers has caused many tickets to be distributed by that company to the deputies, in order to get them to attend the play free of charge, in the expectation of receiving gratuities from the Estates, it has been resolved that a notification shall be posted in the provost's office in the town hall by Loyseau, bailiff of the royal wardens, ordering that the tickets distributed shall be withdrawn and that the deputies, if they elect to attend the play, shall pay admission; inasmuch as the assembly has voted and resolved that it will take no official notice of the company and specifically enjoins the gentlemen of the office of accounts not to make any grant whatsoever to them, directly or indirectly, and also enjoins the cashier of the treasury to make no disbursement to practically no purpose, and to be personally and privately responsible therefor." One of the Béjart brothers had worked out an armorial of the deputies to the Estates. The assembly accepted this tribute with an ill grace, made a grant of five hundred livres to Béjart, and hastened to stipulate that "henceforth it shall bestow no gratuity for such pieces of work except when they have been expressly commissioned." All this begins to savor of mendicancy. It was high time to be casting about for another prince.

The troupe—without Madeleine, who was staying on at Nîmes to try to adjust a legal complication—traversed Provence by way of Avignon, Orange (where Molière fell in with Pierre Mignard, with whom he formed a firm friendship), Lyons, and perhaps Dijon. Then it went on as far as Rouen, the outpost from which it chose to make its overtures for the capture of Paris. Molière's company had now won a name that it was virtually compelled to live up to. It could not appear in Paris unless its claims were resoundingly supported by competent judges and by success. Two courses were open to it: the first, actually to own a theater in order to enter into overt competition with the Hôtel de Bourgogne; the second, to be guaranteed the official patronage of a very influential prince. The two might conceivably be combined; but Molière and Madeleine, whether for reasons of economy or of tactics, chose the second. They had arranged the rental of the Théâtre du Marais—a second-rate, rather nondescript playhouse—when Molière won the patronage of the Duc d'Orléans (the king's brother, generally known as "Monsieur") and gave up the Marais. At this same time history was being made in Rouen. Corneille and his brother Thomas were in love with Marquise du Parc, who inspired the first-named to some famous lines. And when the company finally packed up for the move to Paris the great provincial gave her this appealing and prescient farewell:

Go then, Marquise the fair—to other places turn,
Where still your eyes shall scatter those rays that bless
    and burn.

We shall duly see that there was something of the symbolic in this meeting of Corneille and Molière, but in this context let us keep pace with Molière in his accelerating progress. He had by no means won the patronage of the king's brother without making frequent visits to Paris. "Twice a week," we are told, "there set out from the Rue du Bac [in Rouen] a public conveyance of gothic design, ruggedly built and of somber aspect . . . which reached Paris . . . the third day after its departure." This was the Rouen "Coach." Molière, jolted for hours on end in its ponderous body while mulling over projected scenes of plays or speeches that he was going to address to persons of influence, had no occasion to complain much about his lot. He had attained the topmost rank in the provinces. Paris, to be sure, he had still to win, and he was too well informed to overlook the certainty that the fight would be a redoubtable one.

There were, to begin with, the star actors—grim and leather-lunged guardians of their monopoly or near monopoly of tragic drama. An enemy is truly formidable when ill taste and ill will are combined in him. Molière himself felt confidence in his taste, the merits and the range of his artistic palette; but how was he to convince the city? And then there were all the intrigues that were incessantly forming and dis-

solving at court. If he had to pull wires, he knew how
to go about it—but where was the time coming from?
There was going to be such a multitude of things to
take care of!—discovering what would please the public, and at the same time guiding the public; taking
advantage of the prevailing wind, yet resisting the
wind; asserting himself with enough boldness to make
himself felt, but also with enough discretion to avoid
offense; persuading himself that the approval of great
folk outweighed their whims. There would be, furthermore, all those practical details to arrange, not,
luckily enough, without Madeleine's help—the choice
of a site, the repertoire, the bookkeeping.

"Monsieur" had promised a subsidy; but that was
not to be heavily relied on. The important thing was
to win access to the court and then to gratify Mazarin
and that indulgent young king who was so fond of
the theater. Three days to get to Paris, three more to
get back! Not often again would Molière have the
enjoyment of such six-day interludes, or of the long
industrious holidays of the journeys from city to city.
No longer could he be aware of himself and of other
persons except in the thick of emergencies, collisions,
agitations. Henceforth his life was to consist of losing
his life as a man loses his blood drop by drop through
a tiny wound that will not heal. He was going to
attain renown without the time to enjoy it or even to
inspect it; to drown in fame with bowed head; to
struggle, parry and return blows, and so shape a
world of his own amid shocks of battle and freaks of
fortune, while hewing a path for himself step by step.
They of a later time, in their compassion for what he
endured in his private life, would forget that all his
endurance would be merged into other impulses of his
being to build up an oppressive sense of life in which
endurance frays out into sheer weariness—the kind of
weariness that is not alleviated by happy events, but
merely benumbs a man's realization of them.

Molière's creations so vividly reflect the circumstances of his life in Paris that we catch ourselves

thinking the Molière of the "Coach" must be another man entirely, though we do not contrive to imagine the true inwardness of this stranger. It may be that his dreams were less insistent, his thinking not so tense. It may be that, in that day when the most exalted ideal of mankind was embodied in tragedy, he took pleasure in daydreams of a Molière whose prepotent will should refashion minds and hearts. It may be that after so much bluff rubbing of shoulders with the nameless motley of province and highway he was wondering if he should find this same picaresque background in the city and even at the royal court. And it may be that, beyond the greenery along the Seine, he saw just the dusty main-traveled thoroughfares intersecting as on a luminous map of his yesterdays.

TOWARD TRAGEDY OR COMEDY?

Sage is the King, wills nought beyond attaining.
CORNEILLE

I

WE ARE in the guardroom of the Vieux Louvre. It is October 24, 1658. The court, grouped around the king and Monsieur, is staring at the comediennes whose charms have been proclaimed by the knowledgeable in the provinces. There are three women of voluptuous elegance—the ripening Béjart, the dazzling du Parc, the amiable de Brie; they are coming to Paris to live, and they must be approachable. It is said that the two Corneilles are daft about one of them and that Molière loves all three. Slightly withdrawn and fixed in the rigidity of the judicial process, the actors of the Rue Mauconseil are listening and watching. If they of the Hôtel de Bourgogne are here to criticize, they have at least assessed the occasion as worth the trouble of going out of their way in a body, and that, to Molière, is a kind of victory preceding the defeat that can always ensue—a victory that makes success the harder to attain.

Thalia the mistress of irony, zealous to spare her favorite no single one of her ordeals, has whispered to him that he should play Nicomède—that is to say, the very soul of incarnate self-confidence—in this setting of anguished self-doubt. It is one of the neater tricks to come forward in resolute strides, blurt out those sneering boasts, and string together those lengthy challenges punctuated with curt orders, at the same time perforce watching the king's face out of the corner of one eye, and likewise the faces of Villiers, Poisson, Floridor, Montfleury. *Nicomède*, from beginning to end, holds its sway at those ultimate heights at which it takes either supreme exertion or supreme aptitude to triumph—either a valorous spirit or a wide range of imagination. The prince of Bithynia has nothing left to wish for. He is so securely in possession of his very generosity and his pride that they would serve him merely as promptings to contempt of all mankind, were it not that the accommodations of melodrama modify them into a smile of condescension. Nicomède misses tragedy by being above it: the protagonist here is so superbly armed that he no longer has any adversaries. Nevertheless and despite the corrosive irony of Molière's predicament, the play was a good choice. Of all Corneille's tragedies—and a tragedy it had to be—this was the one that, by virtue of an artless and often intimate style, best lent itself to the resources of an actor who was said to "recite the way people talk." The sturdy, easygoing diction of many of Corneille's passages was perfectly suited to Molière. But there was also the problem of carriage, of general elevation; and this was the more difficult to solve because in Prusias's son sublimity assumed a casual and effortless form.

Molière, without relinquishing an iota of his claims, was well aware that his physical endowments, his gestures, and his presence hardly tallied with people's implicit image of the tragic actor. He was not forgetting the Demosthenean struggles he must have undertaken to improve the distinctness of his voice and to slow down his delivery—struggles that had left a trace in the unfortunate hiccup that he studied to obscure. Mirrors faced him with a rather short body and a disproportionately large and heavy head with a backward thrust, the eyes slightly haggard and as if distended by the exaltation of the looks to which they gave outlet. He walked at a livelier pace than usage approved, and he knew that he did; it was not livelier than he approved himself. It is likely that Molière earnestly believed he was regenerating the art and the style of tragic acting, or rather that he earnestly desired, with his characteristically enterprising boldness, whatever he could himself make of it. But his success depended on others, not on himself. A good actor does not stop at sensing his audience's response: the audience checks him, regulates him, urges him on, all as a danseuse does her partner. And soon his intuitive sense of the public was as much a part of him as his sense of himself. His mind became divided, and thereby he was living on two levels of reality. He was experiencing at the same time something good and something bad, and he could regain his oneness only by either giving in to the audience or making it give in to him. The stage of the theater is only a miniature —or an exaggeration—of the stage that is society. Whoever has an intuitive feeling of people, whether they are scattered or massed, is acquainted with the behaviors of the dual personality; and moralists are letting themselves off too cheaply when they dismiss these behaviors as weakness and vanity.

Did Molière feel, at the end of a performance said to have been no more than passably successful, a variance among the royal personages, the visiting actors, and himself? Had he prepared a surprise in advance for the purpose of showing his company in a new light and with a new justification? In his uncertainty did he want to end on a probable triumph, in the way of an acrobat who erases the memory of a bungled turn by putting on a sure-fire act? If the last possibility was the fact, he made up his mind briskly. This was his day: all these folk had vouchsafed him several hours of concentration. He must keep a tight clutch on his opportunity to the end. Bowing from the waist, right foot forward, knee bent, wig dangling, Molière thanked His Majesty "in the most unassuming terms for His Majesty's kindness in overlooking his faults and those of his whole troupe, which had appeared before so august an assemblage by no means without quaking; he told His Majesty that their desire to afford entertainment to the greatest king on earth had made them overlook His Majesty's having superior originals in his service, of which they were but very inadequate imitations; but that inasmuch as His Majesty had been so indulgent as to bear with their country manners he was very humbly begging His Majesty to permit him to present one of the trifling divertissements that had won him a certain amount of credit and had been found amusing in the provinces." What they acted was the farce *Le Docteur Amoureux*, the loss of which was deplored by Boileau.

It was an astute maneuver. The point was not merely to prove at one stroke the whole range of which the troupe was capable. Although the actors of the Mauconseil had done a good deal with farce before specializing in the serious drama, the red playbills of the Hôtel de Bourgogne were now hardly ever announcing anything but tragedies. The mere fact of "reviving" a divertissement was enough to make it seem titillating to folk greedy of pleasures. Also, this farce may have seemed to promise something beyond itself. Its flexible and unimportant form could be readily extended into the province of ballet; and, so extended, it could contrive a place on the stage for "the greatest king on earth," who was then the most ardent dancer in his kingdom. This wholly unassuming approach, into which Molière suavely slipped a challenge disguised as an apology, aimed at the actors before whom he was humbling himself, shows adequately both his tactical gift and his opportunism. Alceste manages to borrow the demeanor of Scapin.

It was settled that Molière should establish his company in the Théâtre du Petit Bourbon, in the Rue des Poulies, opposite the convent of Saint Germain l'Auxerrois. An Italian troupe, including Scaramouche, was already ensconced there. In consideration of 1500 livres Molière was empowered to act on the off days—Monday, Wednesday, Thursday, and Saturday. These were not so auspicious as the regular days, but the vital point was to get a foothold. The Petit Bourbon had a new, light auditorium under an arched ceiling spangled with fleur-de-lis. The pit tier was graced with Doric columns. In front of the dais reserved for royalty was erected a stage "six feet high, eight toises wide and eight deep"—a little over fifty feet square. The company opened there November 2, 1658.

Because it performed a great many tragedies it has been inferred by some that Molière had intensely coveted the tragic actor's renown—a not impossible thought, even a probable one. It is at first exceedingly difficult to disconnect his name from the word "comedy." Once we have managed it we discover so pointed a contrast between his destiny and those earliest aspirations that we ascribe to him that we take the aspirations to be unarguable. The truth must be more impalpable, harder to define; and in the first place it is imperative to differentiate between what Molière wanted emotionally and what he found practicable professionally. Bear in mind the actor's dual personality and the way his growth depends on the public. Tragedy, at the time when Molière started his campaign, was the most exalted form, the most honored. Comedy amounted to very little—almost nothing. Molière was extremely ambitious. His ambition made him open-minded. He would lean in the direction in which public opinion impelled him; but above all it was a necessity to him to affirm the loftiness and the worth of his claims. It follows logically that he played tragedies, and the best tragedies; but we cannot infer that he approved either their design or their purport. The response of the public was certainly not wanting in candor. Molière apparently achieved no more than a commonplace success until he performed *L'Étourdi* and *Le Dépit Amoureux*. At once the receipts became noteworthy—14,000 francs net profit for the two plays, seventy pistoles to each player. Here was Molière, then, challenged to turn out comedies; and it was wholly natural that he should try to elevate farce to the level of his ambition. As for his secret aspirations, they are another story. On that point we shall in due course ask *Don Garcie* to enlighten us.

At Easter in 1659 there occurred a notable swap-

ping of actors. The du Parcs left the Petit Bourbon
in favor of the Marais—why, we do not know—and
Jodelet and his brother switched from the Marais to
Monsieur's company. Jodelet, who left his signature
on some comedies, was a valuable acquisition. An even
more valuable one was La Grange. He, together with
Du Croisy, was a member of the troupe from then on.
The winsome La Grange, who embodies the ethical
values commonly ascribed to Molière even more completely than Molière himself does—a gentlemanly and
self-restrained Cléante who could allow himself an
easygoing moral code because he punctiliously lived
up to it—was also a sound actor whom Molière paid
the great honor of confiding his secrets to him. La
Grange, on joining Monsieur's company, began scru-
pulously to keep the famous *Registre*, which, with his
introduction to his chief's works, is about the only
important firsthand document we have about Molière.
Along with the de Bries and the Béjarts these new-
comers rounded out a company of some moment, and
one that Molière was able to mold into harmony with
his own style. Du Parc's charms—soon to be restored
to the fold anyway—may for that reason have been
the less missed. Molière was now working out and
putting into shape two radically different types of
comedy: the first, satire masquerading as farce; the
second, a comedy in the heroic strain—a kind of half-
hearted tragedy. The first was already finished, and,
performed far in advance of the second, it may well
have been the determinant of its author's career. The
resounding success of *Les Précieuses Ridicules* is a
milestone in the history, not only of the theater, but
also of French culture.

What first impresses us in the *Précieuses* is the new-
ness of its emphasis; specifically, the welding together
of laughter and meaning. Plenty of plays before this
one had set people laughing, some of them at the same
idiosyncrasies; for example, that very *Cercle des
Femmes* of Chapuzeau from which Molière had derived some ideas, and *Les Imaginaires*, by Saint-Sorlin,

the earliest adumbration of *Les Femmes Savantes*. But improvement in comic understanding had not kept pace with improvement of comedy as a literary form. *Le Menteur*, its sequel *L'Étourdi*, and the love scenes of *Le Dépit Amoureux* succeed delightfully; they are clear-cut, telling, and tautly constructed; but they are not very momentous. The *Précieuses* attains at a bound the comic style that Molière was henceforth merely to modulate and enrich. What that style amounts to is the reduction of speech and gesture to the *only* gestures, the *only* speeches, that give humorous expression to exact meanings. It is a gloriously compact, inevitable, revealing style—a daring simplification that compels us to translate into reflection every convulsion of our laughter. No biography of Molière could contrive to be a treatise on humor, but a biography would be shallow indeed if it did not undertake to extricate the successive conquests of his genius from each of his plays.

Shall we venture to imagine Molière in the act of conceiving the *Précieuses*? If we so venture, we shall begin by imputing a central importance to a particular mood, a particular kind of response in the man, that governs the ideas in this play and extends even to the dramatic devices. Shall we name this mood impatience? To do so would not falsify it, but would leave it vague. Outraged impatience would come a little nearer; outraged impetuosity perhaps nearer still. What we must avoid at any cost is to become the victims of our latter-day point of view by subjecting Molière to a *historical* appraisal of the *Précieuses* and of preciosity. People are certainly going to be telling him before long that he incarnates nature, and he is going to believe it; that he is working in a vein to purify taste, and he is going to keep on doing it harder and harder. And those pronouncements will be true. But the Précieuses, too, incarnate nature; they too have purified taste. We have to go beneath these overrefined notions if we are to trace the hidden instinctive roots of comic insight.

One separate nerve fiber, when it receives a stimu-
lus, will react to it instantaneously with a maximum
intensity that varies hardly at all. Many of our instincts show this inflexible quality; conspicuously the
instincts of sex and of acquisition, which combine in a
feeling of sexual proprietorship that passion will often
arouse in people. Beneath the civilized person is revealed a being more primitive and more imperious—
a being of obstinate, importunate, uncompromising
susceptibilities. The inmost susceptibility of him who
created Arnolphe shows this obstinacy, this primitive-
ness. It vents itself in abrupt releases in which instinct
strives to fulfill itself without indirection and without
remission. This characteristic imparts—to put it into
everyday language—a decided stolidity to character
and temperament, so that they express themselves in
slashing candor, in abrupt breaks. And that impulse
can produce, in the presence of certain exhibitions of
human nature, the outraged impetuosity just mentioned. At this point we perhaps begin to see how
Molière's temper was affected by preciosity. Preciosity is precisely a defensive weapon against the instincts—an elaborate braking mechanism designed to
delay the gratification of them. And delay in any form
was inherently distasteful to Molière. It connotes a
leave of absence, a vacation that one gives oneself, a
margin of independence in relation to the animal in
us. The votary of preciosity has time, or takes time,
or forces others to take their time—especially *his*
time. When instinct is powerful, present in excess, it
can vouchsafe one the luxury of reining oneself in—
the luxury of prolonging or replenishing desire, as
happens in connection with the preciosity in Shakespeare. But it may come to pass, especially with
women, that instinct curbed will wither away; the
vacation becomes a vacancy. The ideas and the language of preciosity—which are one and the same
thing—have ceased to be anything more than an ingenious translation of life's imperatives and have become a license to subvert them. Molière confronting

the Précieuses is insistent instinct—impetuosity in the presence of the frigidity that procrastinates, the elaborate subterfuges that withhold.

Here we undoubtedly have the explanation of Molière's outraged impetuosity, his truculent mood, the ardor that drives him to attack. If his repartee is to attain the comic level, whatever it is that irritates has to be shown as guilty of insufferable inconsistency; for comic vision is not achieved save with the help of reflection. Magdelon, when she proclaims the order of events and the ceremonials of love, exacerbates Molière by undertaking to subject an instinct to a succession of delays, distortions, and calisthenic observances that he finds detestable. But he passes judgment on her, or rather he makes her a figure of comedy, because she is undertaking by all this rigmarole to reduce the flesh to subservience to the mind's dictation and is thinking herself thereby made superior to instinctual man, represented by Molière; and the more subtly because she derives from this spurious idealism an enjoyment that is at bottom sensual, though inverted in such wise that only she gains anything from an intercourse consisting, as far as the instinctual man is concerned, of mere frustrations. From the faces of Cathos and Magdelon we see thus early the cold glitter of Armande's eyes—the eyes of a more consummate and more blameworthy Précieuse.

This deep-rooted feeling—one might almost call it a reflex—seems to us to govern the comic conception of *Les Précieuses Ridicules*. The working-out simply gives it definition and, so to speak, sells it retail. As for the over-all idea of the play, it is clear from the very first that the utmost refinements of preciosity are being dealt with. No one made any mistake on that score, despite Molière's precautions, despite Madame de Rambouillet's good taste. These silly women are, however, decidedly provincial, and not solely for form's sake. In truth, the difference between the précieuses of the provinces and those of the metropolis almost exactly corresponds to the comic distortion

invoked; in other words, *Les Précieuses Ridicules*
could be taken as a realistic depiction of the provincial précieuses and as a comic depiction of the Parisian
précieuses. It is a circuitous device and a diplomatic
one; it is also an artistic device of which Molière was
to avail himself on various other occasions—particularly in *George Dandin*. As for the choice of a plot,
this plot was not new, but we must not overlook the
new coloration imparted to it by the turns of mood
just pointed out. What identifies a great artist is not
solely the power and scope of his painting: it is also
the way in which his subjects, even if common property, derive a fresh and vital enhancement from his
own moods and intensities. The revenge taken by La
Grange and Du Croisy is the revenge of the mere
male with whom the Précieuses decline to go to bed.
And it is Molière's revenge.

Molière's fundamental mood, expressed thus early
in *Les Précieuses Ridicules* and imparting to it a
power absent from the earlier plays, is still without a
trace of bitterness. This comedy is buoyant, unre-
servedly gay, and in the merry ease of its unfolding
the devices resorted to are perhaps more readily detected than elsewhere. At one moment the humor
consists in juxtaposing two versions of the same fact,
one of them ingenuous and coarse, the other elegant;
as when Gorgibus, speaking of his daughter's cosmetic
preparations, grumbles that they have already used up
the pork fat from a dozen hogs. At another moment
the trick is to give the Précieuses speeches in which
they recoil from laying a finger on whatever object
they are mentioning, even on things no more repulsive
than a chair or a mirror. Again, the light will be fo-
cused on "imaginings"—on the fancy for making life
over and daydreaming it according to the conventions
of fiction. (All this sort of thing, too, brings up once
more the recoil from touching anything, the refusal
of contact.) Still again, we get the mutiny of the mere
male, whom we see turned into a critic of diction or
an advocate of reasonableness, as occasion calls for.

The method whereby such criticism is brought to bear shows us a Molière who has completely mastered his craft. He is one of the greatest engineers of comic laughter that have ever lived. We must endeavor to understand how he snatched possession of this effortless power, in that happy period before the comic thrust had penetrated him to the quick.

To take some particular thing seriously means having a conviction of its reality. Having a conviction of the reality of an occurrence that comes to pass under our observation means thinking that the occurrence could not be perceived, seen, or imagined otherwise *at that moment and from that point of view.* A conviction of the reality of an occurrence leads us—still in our role of spectators—to a kind of active participation in its accomplishment; and that means imitation. I have in mind the response that muscles, pulse, breathing, emotions, and thoughts automatically make to an occurrence—a response crudely denoted by some persons' way of making faces and sketching gestures when they listen to a public speaker or an actor. Imitation does not mean approval; getting angry is a sort of imitation, too. The function of laughter is obvious: it is to shatter this harmony with things, this submission to reality.

Such is the result produced by laughter; but how is it brought about? By a hundred devices, every one of which has supplied the makings of a different theory. But all the devices are alike in the effect that they touch off. They abruptly enforce upon us a view of the occurrence different from that suggested by the occurrence itself, and even contradictory to it. Now, we are so constructed that we cannot be aware of a thing in two opposite ways from the same point of view and at the same instant; whence the sensation of slipping and sliding, of tumbling headlong, of swoon, that goes with laughter. Thus the flashes of wit that play over the various meanings of a speech consist in establishing one interpretation of it and then drawing the inferences of a different interpretation, all the while pretending that the first is still operative. For if we are to be made to laugh there must be a dual awareness; a logical impossibility must seem to be the very marrow of the occurrence. This anomaly is found in a graphic form in humor and in irony.

Humor is an ingenious exploitation of the inherent attributes of laughter, especially of its swooning effect, and of what may be called the deflation of reality that ensues from the division of awareness. The comic author undertakes to make use of that instant of startled discomfiture to persuade us of the stupidity or the perniciousness of the occurrence under scrutiny; and he achieves his end with great ease, because the comic impact makes us believe in an impossibility —in the nonexistence of the very thing we are laughing at. To that end he puts before us certain persons and events, then abruptly severs the tie that is forming between them and ourselves. It is at once in the life-likeness of the persons and in the severance of the bond that the secret of comic genius inheres. The problem is one of touch—above all, of timing. Every human reality has indefinable, shifting, tenuous boundaries within which we take it seriously. Once those boundaries are exceeded, the rhythm of identification is lost, we stop participating, we change from actors to spectators, and a critical awareness replaces the immediate awareness of actuality. In this sense comic art is always exaggeration; but it is an exaggeration that must arise naturally out of the thing exaggerated. When Magdelon insists that she would rather have brought forth Mascarille's "Oh, oh!" than an epic poem; when Mascarille, after four iterations of "Stop thief!" crows "Wouldn't you think that that was a man running after a thief to get him arrested?" the utter absence of any poetic transition accounts for the exaggeration needed; but it would lack the comic salt that is in it if it did not surge up out of emotions in the Précieuses that have managed to create an atmosphere of reality. The same principle applies to the

"Come, give us a kiss" that Mascarille addresses to Jodelet, and to the history of Rome couched in madrigals. To establish the rhythm of real life, then stop it dead or overstress it in such wise as to dispel its power of enchantment and to reveal the critical idea that underlies the living palpability—that is the conjurer's trick performed by the genius of comedy.

In the *Précieuses* and in the comedies that were to follow it Molière heightens reality to something beyond itself in order to bring out its blemishes. He modifies facts, then, in a way that will make the exercise of his judgment of them felt. But it must never be forgotten that his judgment respects the life that is in the thing he is disparaging. We might put it that the more implacably he slays in the mind, the more vividly he makes his creatures live in the flesh. Here we have the explanation of those tremendous comic paroxysms, very rare in any age, that his plays suddenly unloose for us. When Magdelon speaks, it is not with any thought of making us laugh; she goes about it in all sincerity, in all earnestness, and this seriousness, underlying the comic intention already made manifest, was incalculably difficult to convey. What she says acquaints us simultaneously with Molière's idea of her and her own idea of herself. The two ideas coalesce on the instant in a unique actuality; there is produced a doubling of our inward vision, as if for an instant we hung suspended between its two halves; and then the abrupt glissade from one to the other provokes our laughter. This sequence shows us why comic genius is in so short supply. It is comparatively easy to impose one's appraisal on the facts, as Voltaire did in order to govern their shape and movement as he saw fit. It is extraordinarily difficult to make characters live, as Molière did—make them live to the marrow—and at the same time to make emerge from what they do the characteristics that condemn them and extinguish them. To accomplish it takes more than critical judgment, more than fancy. It takes the leverage of a mood fully released, the urgency of a vital drama mysteriously finding salvation in the likenesses that it creates.

In *Les Précieuses Ridicules* Molière is still allowing himself pretty much all the licenses of farce; and farce, not having to defer to the plausibility of comedy, lends itself better than comedy does to the bald statement of comic ideas. In it the actor does not forget that he is an actor. The befloured countenance of this one, the mask and the fantastic costume of that one, remind the audience of the appropriate conventions. Molière's entry as Mascarille was stupendous. "Fancy, madame!" Mademoiselle des Jardins records. "His perruque was so big that it swept the floor every time he bowed, and his hat was so tiny you easily guessed that the marquis carried it oftener in his hand than on his head; his bands could pass for a respectable dressing gown, and his breeches trimming looked as if made for nothing but to serve as a hiding place for children playing hide-and-seek; and really, madame, I don't believe the young Scythians' tents were more roomy than that superb breeches trimming of his. A bunch of tassels stuck out of his pocket as if from a horn of plenty, and his shoes were so begauded with ribbons that it is impossible for me to tell you whether they were Russia leather or English cowhide or morocco; anyway I am sure they were a good six inches high, and I was at a loss to imagine how heels so high and so slender could possibly hold up the marquis's body, ribbons, breeches trimming, and powder." Molière had progressed far beyond farce, but it was a mode harmonious with his genius. He loved to paint in broad strokes—in fresco, as he himself said; to proclaim the comic purpose boldly, force the actions and gestures, hurry the pace, and carry laughter by assault. The *Précieuses* is dominated by an atmosphere of comic grandeur that amazes us in a sequence of actions of mock-heroic abruptness, amid all the horseplay and bodily upsets and vibrant repartee. This ludicrous ballet, with its logic shredding out into fantasy, awoke the beholders to a novel pleasure mingled with gratefulness. "Bravo, Molière! that's proper comedy," is the shout attributed to one old man whom one would like to think more than a fiction. His shout is audience repartee.

Some exalted personages were no less affected. Ménage records for us: "I was present at the first performance of Molière's *Précieuses Ridicules* at the Petit Bourbon. Mademoiselle de Rambouillet was there; so were Madame de Grignan and the whole inner circle of the Hôtel de Rambouillet and Monsieur Chapelain and many others known to me. The play was acted to general applause, and for my own part I was so gratified by it that I foresaw at once the effect it was going to have. As we were going out I took Monsieur Chapelain's hand and said to him: 'My dear sir, you and I gave our approbation to all the idiocies that have just been so skillfully and so sagely unmasked; but, believe me—to make use of what Saint Rémi said to Clovis—we shall have to burn up what we have been idolizing and idolize what we have been burning up.'" Possibly Ménage was cultivating in his reminiscences what Jean Paulhan calls anticipation of the past, but his opinion is none the less indicative for that. Mademoiselle or rather Madame de Rambouillet must have taken it all good-naturedly: she was receiving Molière in her own house a few years afterward. And, anyway, preciosity in the special guise at issue was an obsolete refinement. People were grateful to Molière not so much for making it a laughingstock as for confronting it by the same stroke with an art that bade fair to be superior to it. Even so, there was appreciable opposition. One boudoir gallant of high degree, we are told, succeeded in getting the play suspended, and it was not announced again until December 2. What happened in that two weeks' interval? Of that almost nothing is known. Molière must have pulled wires and brought influence to bear. The receipts from the opening performance had been 533 livres; that was only moderate

prosperity, but the brilliance of the critical success
must have made Molière want to repeat the play as
promptly as possible. As a matter of fact, the number
of seats was doubled for the second performance.
The play was put on fifty-three times in less than
two years—something of a triumph for that period.

Meanwhile an adventure befell Molière that is
worth the trouble of chronicling, for it both indicates
the climate of the period and can serve as an index to
Molière's career as author. There was a bookseller
named Ribou who wanted to get a start, and there was
a scribbler named Somaize who was missing no opportunities to get himself into the public eye. The
success of *Les Précieuses Ridicules* gave them an idea
for a fling at bookselling. In January 1660 Ribou
published simultaneously Molière's *Précieuses* and
Les Véritables Précieuses by Somaize. Molière pro-
tested, bestirred himself, and finally obtained a five-
year license. The literary usages of the time forced
him, as a matter of self-protection, to have his play
printed. To this episode we owe the preface in which
Molière complains that he is "not allowed time to
draw breath." "Heavens, the curious predicament of
having a book to get out, and the greenness of an
author never printed before! Moreover, if I had
been granted some time I could have given more
consideration to what I was doing, and I should have
used all the foresight that the writing gentry, now
my fellows, are accustomed to apply to these occasions." How vividly this disheveled and mocking in-
vasion of the literary world, this way Molière has of
assuming a place, all out of breath and unkempt,
among those who are now his fellows, depicts the
man himself and even the quality of the work! It has
all the impudence of Mascarille's intrusion on Cathos
and Magdelon, all the slightly arrogant assurance of
the outsider who knows his worth and is jeering at
the mysteries of the brotherhood. At the same time
it is wary; it promises less than it will be found to
perform; it raises the hope of doing better on the next

attempt. And also—for there is always at least a spark
of fire where there is much smoke—it supplies am-
munition for one kind of criticism that will never
condone Molière's writing a spare, blunt, as it were
hand-hewn style and his making books out of raw
material out of which books are simply not made.

II

Les Précieuses Ridicules had had a Parisian success.
The court was just then preoccupied elsewhere with
negotiating the Treaty of the Pyrenees, and the
opening of the play had been the gainer by the
general outburst of joy when the peace was finally
signed. Molière had appealed to the city for its verdict, and the city had responded with a cordiality to
some extent nonliterary—a cordiality that was from
the heart. He had had his way with the theatergoing
public, won over the most captious judges, and made
everybody perceive that here was the end of an
era. In discussing Molière's merits we must not forget
that he was the eldest of the great, the classic generation and the first to throw down the gauntlet. (I
mean, of course, the first of those whose work is of
major importance; La Fontaine was contemporary
with him.) Boileau, La Fontaine, and Racine followed
him, and he affected all three. As for his enemies, who
were to take the field against him from now on, they
proclaim his stature by turning his own devices against
him. After *L'École des Femmes* their mode of campaign was never to change: they were out to destroy
him, but it was from him that they borrowed their
ideas. The indefatigable Somaize spawned works to
which the word "Précieuse" was essential. A play by
the Abbé de Pure was haled out of oblivion. The sum
of it all was a proof of Molière's prestige. At Easter
of 1660 the du Parcs came back to the "Bourbonnais"
—the players of the Petit Bourbon—and it was probably the success of the troupe that brought them.

On May 28, 1660 the Bourbonnais scored a success almost as great as that of the *Précieuses* and quite

as important if we give due weight to its duration. *Sganarelle, ou Le Cocu Imaginaire* was shown thirty-four times consecutively, with receipts of 350 livres, although the time was that of the king's marriage and the performances ran through the summer. The two successes hand running established a Molière vogue. He had invitations from everybody—court, city, marshals, councilors. He was asked to suppers; he was pressed to do his impersonations, quite as he had been by the Languedoc traders; and, much more valuably from his point of view, he was bombarded with gossipy information and anecdotes about people's idiosyncrasies and morals. Molière was always on wonderfully good terms with the men and women of his time, and they kept him so liberally supplied that he might well be the envy of our latterday devotees of intimate documents. Some invidious commentators will have it that Molière issued these early invitations himself. His doing that would have been a social blunder, though it is conceivable that in the first flush of his triumph he gave in to some naive Jourdainish impulse or other.

Sganarelle shows us a Molière who is making strides. Not that this play is better than the *Précieuses*; but in it he does experiment with new devices, and he does forge ahead toward the rounding out of his craft. His growth as comic actor and manager is integral with his growth as writer for the stage. It is conjectured with some plausibility that he had played Mascarille in a mask. Sganarelle he played without one—his chance to exhibit a command of mimicry that was universally marveled at. The great number of tiny but mobile facial muscles makes facial expression more fleet and more exact than bodily expression, which is always comparatively clumsy and primitive. The face becomes, then, a disembodied epitome of actions and gestures; it gives visible form to impalpable thoughts. Controlled with supreme precision, the play of these accords as well with comedy as with farce. *Sganarelle*, another farce if gauged by its imbroglios and conventional artifices, is composed in delightfully piquant verse. Some fastidious judges do not care for Molière's verse, but I am assured that actors who have it to deliver are of a different mind. The style is concrete—"sturdy," according to Sainte-Beuve—the diction solid; yet it is too elusive for prose—strangely, for it expresses common and tangible things. When Gros-René exclaims: "Pour twenty cups of wine around your heart," the utterance is genuinely poetic. The rhythm of the line accompanies, does duty for, or suggests the rhythm of the corporeal gesture. Voice and thought leap from one line of this outburst to the next as if propelled by springs that send them higher and higher until they "get across" the footlights. Deliver properly Sganarelle's line "Take no offense, my very dear Madame," and you will discover that the "very dear" is by no means just filling—that it by no means denotes a lapse, as you might have thought for a moment when you read it. It touches lightly on Sganarelle's pity at a point where his self-love was more and more in evidence. That line, like any number more, has no empty spaces in it; every syllable of it is mouth-filling. Molière's homely verse is homely everyday speech with its sonorities amplified, so that they reverberate in the mind and affect us as song does.

Molière had not forgotten Ribou: he took out his printing license for the play three days after the first showing. But Ribou had not forgotten himself, either, and he unblushingly got *Sganarelle* printed under an unknown pen name. There was a full-scale lawsuit, with proceedings against the bookseller and the printer and rejoinders from those gentry, before Molière won his point. Meanwhile Doneau had published *La Cocue Imaginaire*. But these two plagiarists, Doneau and Ribou's man of straw, went off at a new tangent by showering Molière with acclaim. And, curiously enough, Molière sanctioned Ribou's edition, embellished with the expository synopses of plot that invariably appear in classical editions.

But the campaign against Molière assumed other forms than these booksellers' stratagems, which were merely ways of cashing in on his commercial value. First the Hôtel de Bourgogne and then the Marais opened hostilities by trying to corrupt the Bourbonnais. Monsieur's actors were repeatedly besought to join one or the other of the rival companies. They remained loyal to Molière; he did not lose a single player. La Grange supplies the very appealing explanation that Molière kept his associates by virtue of his own kindness, his own fairness, and his own genius. To these factors it is proper to add that the Petit Bourbon had become a flourishing business. Also, Molière developed his actors. He made plays for them that fitted their individual talents. Would they have shone with as much brilliance under a different manager and among actors already established and jealous of their privileges? However that may be, and with every concession to La Grange's obituary sentiment, such a consensus of testimony as we have can leave us in no doubt about the kindness that is one of Molière's legendary attributes. I conceive it as a warm friendliness given to bellowing and bullying, but thoroughly just; as a luminous presence that very quickly becomes indispensable; and also as the sympathetic understanding of an intelligence devoid of prejudice—one that, as soon as it is itself again after an outbreak of temper, can perceive no justification at all for others' censure. Molière was an eminently intelligent man with the decidedly and sharply restricted intelligence that is the most valuable asset there can be in a sodality of coworkers; a head foreman rather than an employer—a workman who sets others right by the object lesson of his own work. He was generous, in the way of a man whose giving is the means to his receiving. The fellowship of the theater is no encouragement to ingrowing personalities. Doing everything together, associates in the end learn to know one another. Molière had command of such words as circumvent weariness, irritation, and anger, such half smiles as bestow approval, such fits of depression as can be confessed and can become extraordinarily endearing. Kindness is often nothing but a particular way of sharing confidences.

Molière, secure now in the loyalty of his actors, the privates in his army, had one serious obstacle to overcome. Seemingly without his being able to foresee it, the architects undertook the demolition of the Petit Bourbon in order to enlarge the Louvre. The man who was to add so great a splendor to Louis XIV's reign found himself a sufferer at the hands of fellow craftsmen totally oblivious of him. He had to find a new site, on pain of submitting to an idleness that would have been exceedingly disastrous to a company without many years of success behind it. No evidence better indicates the height to which he had now risen than the way in which he extricated himself from his predicament. He was given nothing less than the auditorium of the Palais Royal, the former Palais Cardinal, on the building of which Richelieu had lavished a special solicitude. Among other distinctions it had a ceiling fashioned on eight beams of such massiveness that their haulage had amounted to 8,000 francs apiece. The auditorium had twenty-seven rows in the pit and two gilded balconies. Most important of all, the mechanical apparatus was of a greatly improved sort. To obviate idleness while the work of refitting went on, Monsieur's troupe put on a good many "guest performances"— showings at the residences of personages, often for large fees. At last, on January 20, 1661, it was possible to dedicate the auditorium in which Molière was to present his masterpieces.

It was with no masterpiece that he began, although he himself appears to have thought otherwise. Among the unlaunched craft that Molière had had on the ways since his arrival in Paris there was one play to which he had devoted the most loving care. He had been giving readings of excerpts from it from the time of *Les Précieuses Ridicules*. On May 31, 1660 he had listed it among the works for which he was applying for a license. In the end, very significantly, it was with this play that he chose to initiate his performances at the Palais Royal. It was not a comedy, although its hero was another imaginary cuckold; nor was it a tragedy. It was called *Don Garcie de Navarre, ou Le Prince Jaloux*. Its reception was to be a disappointment to Molière. It dragged its painful way through seven showings; the 550 livres that he collected made one fifth of the total receipts. It is thought that he discontinued the performances out of considerateness, in order not to inflict material injury on his associates. Later on he enacted *Don Garcie* at court, and there it was found more acceptable. But from the end of 1663 he gave it up for good and all, salvaging from it no more than some very effective lines that he was to distribute among sundry other comedies, especially *Le Misanthrope*.

This setback to Molière's aspirations ought to detain us briefly. *Don Garcie*, which Molière had been fond of and had wrought with care, and on which he had unquestionably staked much, is an extremely revealing work. From it we can extract some valuable information, no less about the man than about his talent.

Picture to yourself an actor thoroughly acclimated to playing Corneille. (A Corneille tragedy had been used as companion piece to every one of the new comedies that Molière had put on since settling in Paris.) This actor is also an author who can conceive no higher pinnacle of tragedy than that attained by Corneille; and he is a manager to whom Corneille's characteristic approaches are among the integral appurtenances of tragedy. Granted that this man is endowed with a temperament and a history as remote from those of Corneille as could be, and granted that his temperament prevails over his prudence, he works out a play of the "serious" order to which action on the pattern of Corneille and interpretation on the pattern of Molière both contribute, each after its kind. The result is a flawed conception, a dearth of solidity and of inevitability. It does not cover the case to call *Don Garcie* a weak play: it is a play that baffles understanding, a play that fails to justify its existence for the reason that the values out of which it contrives its effects are mutually contradictory.

Elvire, the heroine, is a Corneille heroine; she and Pauline are, so to speak, kissing cousins. The heart, she declares, is always within our control, and if sometimes it betrays a certain weakness, reason must assert its sway over instinct. She therefore requires to be as much respected as loved by Don Garcie; that is, she requires to be loved "as one ought to be loved." The best proof of respect is to trust the beloved person. Elvire demands that, regardless of appearances, Don Garcie shall believe in her. Now, the precise point is that Don Garcie is not in the smallest degree a Corneille hero; and the major interest of the play derives from its exhibition of what manner of man was Molière's imaginary hero in a serious relationship. Don Garcie is a jealous man; that is, a particular passion natural to his temperament is stronger in him than all considerations of reason and of respect. In Corneille's code jealousy is an offense against love; it devours both the beloved and the lover, gives animal nature ascendency over human nature, and above all severs every tie between love and the exalted principles of the human ideal. Thus, Don Garcie comes to seem an intruder into a world of which he is unworthy, or a spoiled child who is being overindulged —as Don Sylve makes him feel by a harangue in the style of Nicomède—and when Elvire, disguising her fondness under an engaging irony, tells him that she yields to his pleas out of pity, we are tempted to take her more seriously than she is taking herself. But what we cannot manage to take seriously—and this is an even more crucial matter—is that elevated, that supernal world. The fire and the grandeur of Corneille are missing. Corneille is great not because he is sublime, but because his sublimity is genuine. Molière's is chill; it is abstract. It is a lesson that Elvire recites, and that in a style of traditional abstract figures of speech not at all matched by any inner ardor in the character who utters them. One does not see how this play—a play about a man unworthy of the woman he loves and a woman insufficiently vital to vindicate this contrast in worth—could have attained to any true balance.

The truth is that an art cannot stand upright without the support of some ethical system—one whose exact purport matters little provided it answers to the personality of the artist. In *Don Garcie* there are two ethical systems that quarrel. Nothing could be more illuminating in this connection than a comparison of *Don Garcie* with *Le Misanthrope*. Remember that many lines of the earlier play were inherited by the later, and with them one scene almost *in toto*—that in which the misled lover rages against the object of his passion. In *Don Garcie* these passages are already fine, but they crop up without pretext and lead to nothing. *Le Misanthrope* puts them where they belong. It is in this play, we should notice, that the true drama is enacted. A man jealous without a shadow of excuse would be unendurable on the stage: therefore Don Garcie has to be provided with pretexts, and these smell of contrivance. And yet it is *Le Misanthrope*, serious as it is, that is the genuine comedy. The explanation of this seeming paradox is not very elusive. From beginning to end of *Don Garcie* we sense that Molière does not love Elvire, whereas throughout *Le Misanthrope* we sense that he does love Célimène. The acknowledged fact that we do not love whom we choose to love, and that it sometimes takes the least worthy woman to arouse the most single-minded passion, was calculated to modify Molière's ideas about life and consequently the basic terms of his expression of them. At the time we have now reached he seems not yet to have become aware of this truth, and that is why his hand faltered and his inventiveness was without warmth. Elvire is a high-minded lady and frequently sublime, but she does not move us at all. And her sublimity moves us even less than anything else. Fundamentally, in this bad play there is proclaimed the divorce between the spirit of Corneille and the spirit—anyway, one spirit —of the new age that Molière and his fellows were to embody; a spirit that comprised exploration of the rational basis of the passions, the reasoning faculty applied to studying man rather than to idealizing him, moderation, skepticism, detestation of the romantic, and a lenient judgment of the promptings of instinct. The failure of *Don Garcie* points to something like a need of release from an interpretation of life out of harmony with the inward experience of it. On what are Racine's plays built if not on the irrelevance to love of ideal considerations? Molière is not so uncompromising as Racine. He belongs to a generation midway between the author of *Cinna* and the author of *Andromaque*, and he clings to a basic idealism, a propensity to indignation, and a need to reform things. He is one of those persons who, to feel themselves excellent, have to fume at ridiculous folk or wrongdoers. Also, his moralizing idiom is that, not of serenity, but of irascibility. The moral illumination that does not seem direct and searching except as it is encompassed by heavy, grotesque shadows is the very nucleus of the comic temper. Elvire is far too noble to permit Don Garcie's disposition to find its proper key, its justification, and its real meaning.

The fate of *Don Garcie* delivers an unequivocal answer to the question that heads this chapter. The interpreter of *Nicomède* is not himself in the raiment of tragedy. Does someone object that it was the cut of the raiment that did not suit him, and that a new pattern would have done him credit? It is not apparent that he could have fitted himself to either better than to the other. In any event no evidence entitles us to imagine that he could have. Molière's striving was not to attain the level of the higher tragedy, but to elevate comedy to a level as high as that of tragedy. Through the ensuing years he was never to let that goal out of his sight. His striving, together with the marvelous ease of his perfecting a consummate comic apparatus, convinces us that tragedy was not his vehicle for expressing himself. And there were other compulsions that restricted him to comedy—among them his physical build and his range of facial expression. I am well aware that he had already tried, and would persistently keep on trying, to make people think his company played tragedy better than the Grands Comédiens did; but who will maintain that so fastidious an artist as Racine chose the Hôtel de Bourgogne over the Palais Royal for no reason but to play a dirty trick on his friend?

To be sure, it is possible to look at the matter in a different light—one that reveals rather the man than the writer and interpreter. Molière's chronic depression is hardly less well attested than his kindness. In Scarron's *Pompe Funèbre*, when Molière is proposed as Scarron's successor, the author tells Molière that he is "an oversententious clown." Michaut sees in that speech an offensive reference to *Don Garcie*. I should see in it, rather, either a reference to the "sententious Molière," in the class of references to "Molière the observer" and "Molière the thinker," or else a pronouncement on the critical turn imparted to the *Précieuses* and on the scope that it undertook to add to comedy. It must not be forgotten that comedy was a mode as yet but little esteemed and that the prestige of tragedy in the vein of Corneille relegated comedy to the second rank, not to say the third. It would seem pretty difficult to plumb the depths of the human heart in a work meant to evoke laughter. Molière, by dint of the leverage of his own experience, his alternate exuberance and discouragement, the clarity and the gravity of his thinking, was to plumb those depths, and to do it again and again. He may very well have been mistaken about the form that he was to impose on what he had to say. He was undoubtedly inspired to begin with by models that

suited him but ill. At the same time, in order to meet
the public demand, swell the volume of receipts, and
keep on exploiting a form in which he shone without
competition, he was perfecting his comic idiom. Possibly he was not then clearly aware that the great
serious works he was pondering would achieve their
perfect realization in that very idiom and no other.
But the time was not far off when the master of
comedy and the master of tragedy, put asunder in
conventional tradition, were to coalesce and be in-
dissolubly one in their approach to life. And, now
that we have been spectators of this tremendous beginning, we reach the moment for drawing nearer to
the human being behind the plays, in an effort to
discover in his own and others' proclivities the living
springs of his genius.

CHAPTER FOUR

THE FORWARD MARCH OF COMEDY

We have to thank thy mirthful muse
For truth that all the world can use.
Thy school will never fail to teach;
For all therein is fair and good,
And often thy most flippant speech
Says all the sagest sermon could.

BOILEAU

IN 1661, about Easter, Molière asked his associates to assign him two shares of the profits—a fact confirmed by La Grange in his *Registre* in a marginal notation of uncertain date: "For him or for his wife if he should marry." Molière was actually to be married nine months later, on February 20, 1662. He was to marry Armande Grésinde Claire Élisabeth Béjart, about whom it is not known with absolute certainty whether she was the sister or the daughter of his former mistress Madeleine.

Molière's fondness for Armande is shown by a letter that Chapelle wrote him during the vacation season in 1659:

"Truth to tell, my very dear friend, but for you I should scarcely have thought of Paris this long time, and I shall not be able to make up my mind to withdraw until the sun does. All the charms of the countryside will only increase and improve from now on, especially the greenery; the trees will be leafing out one day soon, and we are beginning to find fault because the heat is making itself felt. It will not be oppressive right away, though; and for this excursion we shall have to be satisfied with what carpets the ground (the verdancy, the verdure), which, to describe it to you in slightly more exalted terms,

> Young and tender, through the meads
> Creeps, but lacks the strength it needs

74

To pierce and tinge the willow tree
That, reaching for it yearningly,
With outheld arms in silence pleads.

The amorous tree, the while it spies
These nascent beauties, only bleeds
Its tears of sap and, envious, sighs
For what along the meadow lies;
But in six days or five, it vows,
The same shall gild its topmost boughs.

"You will show these fine lines to Mademoiselle
Menou and no one else, so felicitous an image are
they of her and you.

"As for the others, you will perceive well enough
the specific advisability of not letting your women-
folk see them, both by reason of their content and
because . . . they are as bad as could be. I concocted
them by way of comment on the part of your letter
that goes into details about the annoyance given you
by your three great actresses' resentments over your
assignments of parts. I must get back to Paris so that
we can work it out together and, while doing our
best to succeed in matching your parts to their personalities, allay this strife that bothers you so. Indeed,
O man of parts, you have need of all your brains for
the guidance of theirs, and I liken you to Jupiter
during the Trojan War. . . ."

This Mademoiselle Menou—there is no occasion to
doubt that she was Armande—had already appeared
as a mere child, or at least her name had appeared, in
Corneille's *Andromède* at Lyons in 1653. It is more
than a little ironic to catch sight of her through this
sensuous figure of speech, in an involvement at once
conjugal and filial. But inasmuch as there is no ap-
proaching this marriage of Molière save with extreme
wariness, Chapelle's bucolic letter is a clear challenge
to pause for contemplation of Molière's feminine environment—the trio of actresses that encircled him.

Molière never had a steady everyday friendship
with anyone of his own sex. Chapelle, La Fontaine,
Boileau, and Racine were rather fellow men of letters

than friends, some of them more and some less close to him. Louis XIV could not be any man's friend, even if he had wanted to be. Baron was to bring into his mentor's life some gifts quite other than those of friendship. Such men as Rohault and Mignard, for whom Molière apparently had the most cordial fellow feeling, pursued occupations so remote from his that only occasionally was he able to share with them his worries and his opinions. His associate La Grange is undoubtedly the one man with a valid claim to be called his faithful day-in-and-day-out friend. But La Grange was rather the ideal coworker than the confidant and object of deep affection. Molière, with him, unburdened himself of one division of his troubles with the complete trust that a man owes to a tested assistant, but, La Grange's attributes being what they were, Molière could hardly use intercourse with him as a means of getting his mind off his profession. And what he appears to have sought now and then, in the midst of the variegated outpourings of fortune that we associate with him, was surcease from his occupation, surcease from his worries—the outlet of a man momentarily set free. Having no friend, he had to make the best of himself and of the women of his group.

These he was seeing every day, every hour, on every sort of occasion—through the day for assignment and rehearsal of parts, through the after-dinner performances, through court performances in the evening, at suppers and during visits, and after it all in nocturnal intimacies of the flesh. For women alone furnished him with possibilities of escape and of release from tension. But there was no friendship in this. His escape was such as must forge additional chains for him. Chapelle mentions squabbles—certainly as common among actresses as among society women or nurses—and it is no strain to imagine that the "matching" of parts to the actresses' personalities involved touchy and provocative considerations having to do with these young women's ages and qualifications. And it is not too easy to conceive that this professional diplomacy never got mixed up with Molière's personal relationships with his stars, or that any professional observation might not readily come to betoken a quite different category of feelings. Molière was, in fact, the lover of at least two of his stars, and his relationship to the third, Mademoiselle du Parc, is not embarrassed by any surplus of transparency.

Madeleine Béjart was no longer the beloved, dominant, contented woman of twenty years earlier. Still magnificent on the stage, she may have lost something of her intimate seductiveness. Anyway, we have no knowledge whatever whether Molière wearied of her or she of him—a possibility to which biographers have given inadequate consideration. For, when all is said, her unremitting zeal for Molière's prosperity is by no means enough to prove that she loved him. A woman of brains, serious about money, treasurer and co-manager of the company, she had a function as business partner that imposed on her a bond quite strong enough to give her every appearance of an emotional attachment. She seems to have been always easygoing and anything but strait-laced on the score of her love affairs. The primmest of her biographers do not entirely dismiss the notion that at several intervals of her liaison with Molière she may have renewed her relations with Monsieur de Modène. Some of them, it is true, have ascribed to her in connection with Molière's marriage all the furies and tantrums of the deserted mistress; but others have as freely ascribed to her the small connivances of a matron well content to secure the future of her illegitimate daughter or favorite sister. Whatever the fact, Molière thoroughly respected her, and it may have been as much for her sake as for his own that he stuck to acting tragedies. What part she played in the altercations referred to by Chapelle, we do not know. Was she experiencing the stale odors of jealousy? Was she dramatizing a simulated jealousy in order to gratify a genuine artistic ambition? Or, indeed, was she reclaiming through her actress's emotionalism some of the exorbitant demands of the young woman to whom nothing could be denied?

Catherine de Brie, who was shortly to have the distinction of translating the incomparable Agnès into flesh and blood for the seventeenth century and for future generations, is fairly difficult to become acquainted with. She it was who, under the name Catherine de Rosé, at Narbonne in 1650, held a baby at the baptismal font at Molière's side. It is believed that she did not become her manager's mistress until about when the company settled in Lyons, not far from the time when Molière is supposed to have been rebuffed by du Parc. Unfortunately, this last statement is but hearsay. We do not know whether Molière actually fell in love with Thérèse de Gorla, or whether he was scorned or accepted; all we know is that he was very amorously inclined and she very beautiful. Catherine de Brie was tall and rather slender, with a face that was pretty enough and doubtless more pleasant than pretty. Her deportment was gentle and reserved. Molière willingly saved the ingénue parts for her—an evidence, not that she had innocence, but most likely that she had adroitness and brains. It is commonly insisted that she served Molière as a consoler whose ungrudging kindness alleviated his difficulties, but we know nothing about it. She appears to have been most gracious in the ultimate intimacies and practically devoid of coquettish wiles. She was the wife of the de Brie who was one of Molière's pet aversions; Molière bestowed the repellent roles on him as an outlet for his own spleen. At the time of Chapelle's letter Catherine was still Molière's mistress, as indeed she was to be until a few months before his marriage. She was a first-rate comedienne and a flexible instrument from whom Molière drew a variety of effects. For her he saved, too, the prudish roles and the intricate task of creating Armande in *Les Femmes Savantes*.

Mademoiselle du Parc has no direct share in the intimate side of Molière's life, although (as we have conjectured in citing the Abbé de Cosnac's account) she may have been an object of his desire. Of the three stars she is unquestionably the most complicated, and she corresponds the most exactly to the generalized idea of a capricious beauty. This so-called second Helen, accustomed as she was to every sort of accolade, was marked for a more tragic fate in more senses than one. (She was to die young; Racine was observed to weep at her funeral; and there was a current rumor that she had been poisoned.) Racine was shortly to discover her and to bring about her transfer to the Hôtel de Bourgogne, where she played men's parts and roles calling for brazenness—beplumed Dorimènes. Her presence must have contributed no little to the spread of unrest and tension. And it may be that she decided to reap the profits of an intimacy with Molière that she had once declined.

Around Molière these three Graces conducted in mutual enmity their stately, tedious sarabande. It is rare enough for any woman to make the most of the passive leverage of friendship, to say nothing of actresses who are doubling as actual or potential paramours, all of them obsessed with their own ambitions. If by chance any one of them did Molière the kindness to think of him for his own sake, it was *only* by chance and as a transient interlude in a precarious liaison. These half mutinous soldiers can hardly pass muster as "the warrior's surcease." What, after all, were they—these three women? Madeleine, the most reliable of them, had had only lovers in her life. Catherine de Brie's husband was at the best a numskull, at the worst a pander. It is said that Gros-René was beloved by the second Helen, but what a dismal tale that is—or what a mockery! Molière, it may be, pictured marriage as a clear-cut antithesis to the relationships with which he was familiar—as placid love in clear-cut contrast with his amorous entanglements and the memories of his own love affairs; and not

merely, as has been asserted, in moral revulsion or as a
recrudescence of middle-class respectability, but above
all else as a consequence of his sensuality. The impulse
of sexual proprietorship that we have ascribed to him
may well have been asserting itself at this point. Virginal freshness, vernal emotions, and submissiveness
make a beguiling contrast with promiscuity, even if
we grant that Armande was not exactly an innocent.
And it is a purifying contrast, too. Molière, by his
innate disposition and his natural habits enslaved to
the influence of women, could attain self-renewal only
through a woman completely new to him. Rooted as
he was in instinct and the life of the senses, he was
probably incapable of reaching purification except
through some species of excitement. And, after all,
what better way was there of escaping recklessness
and restlessness than by taking charge of his own
well-being? Whence the aside that Chapelle introduced, which gives his letter all its meaning and its
charm.

But irony, Molière's unfailing attendant, prompted
him to seek salvation and orderliness amid confusion
unlimited. Anything connected with the Béjart clan
seems irreducible to middle-class requirements. Mademoiselle Menou—Armande, the tender verdure, the
flower of the family—has such mysteries connected
with her paternity, her birth, her civil status, as lend
color to the most appalling suggestions. With the best
will in the world and the least disposition to fictionize,
one can assert nothing about Armande that is not in
the domain of enigma and likely always to remain
there. And the enigma is extremely revealing by virtue
of its very mysteriousness.

Until 1821 tradition accepted Armande, with hardly
a dissent, as Madeleine Béjart's illegitimate daughter.
This tradition was supported by the conviction and
the declarations of contemporaries of Molière, and
primarily of his friends. Brossette records: "Monsieur
Despréaux told me that Molière had been in love in
the first place with the comedienne Béjart, whose

daughter he had married." In 1821 Beffara found the original of Molière's marriage certificate, in which Armande is stated to be daughter to Marie Hervé, spouse of Joseph Béjart and Madeleine's mother. In 1863 Eudore Soulié discovered a petition for relinquishment of rights to an inheritance from Joseph Béjart by Marie Hervé, dated 1643, in which among Marie's children is mentioned "a baby not yet christened." Clearly, in the absence of Armande's baptismal certificate, which is undiscoverable, the 1643 document is the only one that should engage our attention. An actual or alleged falsification of the parents' ages has cast doubt on its veracity. It has been surmised that Madeleine ascribed to her mother an infant of her own. The problem is complicated by the fact that Madeleine actually bore in 1638 an infant named Françoise of whom no later trace is found. Whether Françoise renewed her infancy under the name Armande, or whether Madeleine had a second baby in 1643, a substitution would not have been in any wise impossible. A point cited in substantiation of it is the dowry of 10,000 livres that Marie Hervé—who was penniless—settled on Armande; it could only have come out of Madeleine's resources or Molière's. It is pointed out, too, that the godfather of Molière's second child was Comte Esprit de Modène, that its godmother was Madeleine, and that this infant was christened Esprit-Madeleine. Finally, a point is made of Molière's own silence and of the absence of doubt among the persons the least inclined to wish him ill.

Innuendoes were not lacking during Molière's lifetime, and there were more than innuendoes. At the height of the altercation with the Grands Comédiens Montfleury's son addresses to Louis XIV a petition in which Molière is charged with marrying the daughter after having cohabited with the mother; at least, such is the straightforward account given by Jean Racine. After Molière's death, at the time of the Lully-Guichard trial, Guichard's lawyer reproached Armande for having been her husband's daughter and her father's wife. In *Élomire Hypocondre* (1670) Élomire (Molière) avers that he had "forged" a wife for himself from before the cradle. That Molière got this "infamous work" suppressed merely proves his standing, not the justice of his claim. Nevertheless, why challenge the authenticity of documents that antedate the legend contradicting them? Was not Madeleine, after losing Françoise, able to show the solicitude for Armande that would befit a daughter of her own? And her settling on Armande a dowry of 10,000 livres, her making Armande virtually her sole residuary legatee—may not these benefits have been earmarked for Molière's wife, Molière's family? and may not Madeleine have been staking a great deal, as Molière himself was doing, on the auguries of orderliness and of middle-class respectability that this marriage connoted? Just so, but the documents may contain falsifications; but there remains the apparent certainty of Molière's friends; but—and so on. Since it is still possible that Molière had fathered Armande, those who hold by the belief that Armande was Madeleine's daughter thereby debar themselves, whether or no, from acquitting Molière of the charge of incest. For one of the reasons behind the false ascription of maternity may well have been that Molière was the father. The idea may have been considerateness of Monsieur de Modène's sensibilities, or it may have been the young lover's own discomfiture over a baby so come by. The truth is that if you trust the documents there is no explaining away the assertions of Molière's contemporaries—assertions that he himself never contradicted. And if you trust to the legend that obtained up to 1821, it cannot be categorically denied that Molière's marriage may have been an incestuous one.

We can, in fact, take it as a certainty that the private lives of Molière and the Béjarts were most disorderly if measured by our ordinary moral standards. In that society and its contiguous circles codes of morals were then no better stabilized than the spelling of proper names or the Frondeurs' patriotism. I will merely cite as example the analogous story of our friend Modène and the L'Hermites of Vausselle, who had spent an interval as part of Molière's company in the provinces. Monsieur de Modène became the lover of the wife of Jean Baptiste L'Hermite, who had been godfather to Françoise Béjart; then, at something over sixty, Modène married the daughter of this same Jean Baptiste. His doing so leads one to believe that this episode has left its imprint on the parallel one—that what has come down to us is a composite picture. But the best way to extricate ourselves from this labyrinth is, after all, by trying to recover the mental state of the period. A mania for building, for organizing, and a contempt for history are equally characteristic of those years. Louis XIV's people had not a smattering of our persuasion that a river amounts to nothing unless its source has been discovered. To them the clean slate was something more than a theoretical expedient. In that frantic forward march of French society what was achieved counted a great deal more than the origins of those who achieved it. To the man of that era the years of his youth looked like a mere senseless, half unreal tossing about. He turned his back on those years, and if he had not himself felt an antipathy to them, the trouble of cajoling the sovereign would have imposed oblivion of them. It is probable that this social state of mind had its repercussions in the private feelings of Louis XIV's subjects. A man certainly bore the stamp of his early years, but he made a fresh beginning from where he stood, and he had to prove what he was by what he did. Truth came from the king, not from analysis of the past. Thence arose the revulsion against recapitulating one's own story, inasmuch as its disorderliness had no bearing on the wish for present orderliness; thence the focusing of attention on the present and the reliance on the future that may to some extent account for Molière's attitude.

The facts about Armande's girlhood are no clearer

than those of her origin. She is said to have been
brought up in the provinces, at least until 1653, perhaps by those same L'Hermites of Vausselle. In 1661
she was a tall, rather skinny girl with a large mouth,
a prominent nose, small eyes, and hair of great fineness
caught up on a slender neck—the type of woman that
can be bewitching precisely because her appeal is not
bound up with too standardized perfections. As we
have noted, it has been asserted among other contradictory assertions that Madeleine had astutely thrown
Armande in the way of her own former lover. She is
supposed to have coached Molière to realize "the
satisfaction that there is in bringing up for oneself a
child whose affection one can count on possessing and
whose disposition is known to us." Whether it was
she or Molière who said this, and whether during a
spat or during a cosy talk, Molière probably reckoned
on the intimate knowledge and the possession specified. He did not know much about young girls; and
inasmuch as young girls do not know much about
themselves, there were no mistakes whatever that
Molière might not commit in his interpretation of
Armande's attitude, even if we credit her with the
best of intentions. It appears, moreover, that Molière
felt weighed down with uneasiness and hesitancy before this stranger, despite a self-confidence not in
the least simulated. Men are not simple creatures, and
Molière was not the simplest of the breed. Two great
comedies, one preceding and the other following his
marriage very closely—*L'École des Maris* and *L'École
des Femmes*—throw a curious light on the state of his
heart and mind. True, it has been denied that Sganarelle, Ariste, and Arnolphe have any correspondence
whatever with Molière; but to say so amounts to
denying criticism and, together with criticism, the
license to fathom creative works and to discover their
bearings on the life of their author. And since one of
the considerations that differentiate a dramatic masterpiece from a mediocre work in the same form is

its vital importance to him who re-creates it, such a rejection amounts to denying our license to exalt a great artist above other men.

L'École des Maris was shown for the first time on June 24, 1661. Molière wrote it about the time when he was making up his mind to marry—undoubtedly the reason for the innovations that he added to a classic subject. It is a suggestive fact that Terence's *Adelphi*, the immediate source of Molière's inspiration, has to do not with conjugal education, but with paternal. Into this reshaped matrix Molière poured a completely personal, completely intimate feeling. The instinct of ownership is not too remote from the paternal instinct, and no man need be incestuously given to feel as the father of a much younger woman whom he has reared for himself.

Maurice Donnay has prettily called this comedy "a betrothal play," in reference to Ariste's sensible advice, whereby he wins Léonor's affection. We acknowledge, to be sure, that Ariste is Molière's mouthpiece, and Sganarelle a bogy designed to accentuate the moral attractiveness of a man older than himself. But it seems to me that here Sganarelle means something deeper and more complex. For an understanding of how Molière's sentimental subject manages to generate the comic subject of *L'École des Maris* it is pertinent to note that the sympathy between Ariste and Léonor undoubtedly delineates the ideal relationship that Molière was projecting for himself and, most important, for his wife-to-be; that Armande was probably intended to play Léonor; and that Molière kept the part of Sganarelle for himself. No doubt he had already decided on that use of himself, and his mimetic gift marked him for it. But that is not the whole story. Ariste is an old man, and Sganarelle, who is of an age with Molière, is comparatively youthful and does not fail to make the most of the fact. If, then, Ariste captures the love of Léonor, what might we not think possible to an

Ariste disburdened of twenty years? It is extremely
adroit of Molière to make the impression of age conveyed by Sganarelle a consequence of his own inclination, the propensity of his own make-up, in such
wise as to impart a telling emphasis to Ariste's youth-
fulness. Nor is it for nothing that Molière puts Sganarelle into garments of a bygone fashion. The victory
of reasonableness in *L'École des Maris* might very
well be simply the astute formulation of a wholly personal self-defense.

And thus much is still not the whole story. Between
Molière and Sganarelle we detect some genuine if
disguised resemblances. I have remarked on the abruptness, the quasi-unwieldiness, of Molière's feelings and
impulses, his tendency to drive straight to the mark,
to live in spurts, forthrightly. His discretion is only
an afterthought, oftentimes an ideal—the product of
a searching reconsideration that exerts no great control over his rather unreasoning impulses; a kind of
consoling daydream that fascinates his mind without
emancipating his emotions. For this reason it is extremely rash to gauge Molière's "morality" by the
sententious harangues that he puts into the mouths of
his dialecticians. That morality is an ideal, but it is a
static ideal that would seem completely inert if it did
not encounter the counterstrokes of passionate instinctual actions that gainsay it. And these instinctual actions issue from Molière as from an inexhaustible
living spring. If his reason gainsays his temperament,
it is that temperament that accounts for the livingness
of his work; and it is evident that, under the auspices
of a plot that passes judgment in advance on the
uncompromisingness and arbitrariness of that temperament, Molière as an actor was finding his release,
purging himself if you like—in any event thoroughly
appeasing himself—by exaggerated expression of his
inmost propensities.

With the play written and rehearsed, Molière put
on "the long doublet, very long and fastened to a

nicety," tightened the ruffle around his neck, and
stepped on to the lighted stage. He was calm; mind
and conscience were serene. His fellow players knew
their parts. The mimic fate of each had been predetermined in conformity with trustworthy rational
considerations. Armande, in an angle of the wings,
was about to receive the lesson that she would one
day put into practice. Molière was calm. His "philosophy" was to be recited to a thronging audience and
to do battle for his own happiness. Sganarelle was
doomed: good sense would have it so, Molière had
decided it so. But until he is blown to bits in the comic
explosion he is going to live—live with all he has in
him, live to surfeit; and it is with Molière's life that
he is going to live—with Molière's very muscles and
blood and ardency. He will assert his tyrannical
ownership of the woman, his implacable determination
to understand no manner of speech but his own, to
stay wrapped in his own inconsistencies. He will surrender himself to the delightful but fatal sloth of
being exactly all that he chooses to be, perfectly aware
the while that he is as far as possible from what he
really wants to be. Molière, to be sure, is not Sganarelle; but a lot of Molière's blood has got over into
Sganarelle's bloodstream. I should say that anyone
who fails to understand this self-surrender under the
mask of a synthetic wisdom fails to understand the
whole Molière—the whole meaning and the whole
power of his comic art. Into the still indecisive argument over the autobiographic import of *L'École des
Maris* I shall interject, then, the following observations: (1) The theme of the play discloses Molière's
anxieties about marital life and particularly about marital education. (2) In the degree that the play can
exert any practical leverage it amounts to a warning
and a defense *in behalf of Molière* rather than of
Armande. (3) For him, primarily and finally, it constitutes an expression of himself through a pure poetic
fantasy in which his quarreling propensities achieve

the reconciliation of a comic accord. For autobiography, aesthetically considered, can hardly mean anything other than transference of a person to a plane not commonly practicable.

The comedy was a thumping success. Molière's genius was visibly expanding. His salutary gift was beginning to satisfy the inveterate need of thoughtful laughter—a need as acute as, for the most part, ill supplied. The play is rich in attributes either new or better realized. At the head of them is the striking parallel between the plot and the minds of the characters; the unfolding of the plot corresponds with the relationships among them. Next, there is the forthright candor of the preliminary exposition. The opening act makes clear the rules of the game and the motivations; the rest is but the working out. But what a working out! Molière extracts a wonderful range of effects from the spoken exchanges—variegated exchanges, now copious and now meager, and each evoked by the preceding; exchanges varied in intensity with a musical accuracy in their shadings; retorts neatly "planted" in a way to give them their maximum impact, whether under the pressure of the speeches immediately preceding or by interplay of transition scenes marked by the "timing" of gymnastic evolutions. The words cease to be mere words and become forces obedient to the laws of mechanics; the scenes cease to be something written, or even something acted, and are projected into space and abandoned to a development as inexorable as the swings of a flying trapeze.

Sganarelle dominates it all, as he propels it all. The leap from Mascarille to Sganarelle is a tremendous one. Mascarille made others laugh; and when he was laughed at he knew it. Sganarelle does not know that he is comic or what is the source of his power—the power of inanimate objects that spare nothing. In this state he inflicts all manner of punishment on himself, but he does not know it, for he is oblivious and blind. Shut up in his self-centeredness as in his doublet, he

sprays contempt on the world. But he is bound to
the world by cords that are shortly to be drawn
tight. The bond is by no means love, for—as Jacques
Copeau saw clearly—he does not love Isabelle at all.
The bond is self-sufficiency. Therefore, as soon as
anyone shows him a picture of himself that caresses
his vanity he goes vigorously ahead with absolute
assurance and simplicity, and his going ahead is the
making of the play. This time it is the character as a
whole that brings about the dual awareness that we
have found to be the quintessence of comedy. Completely out of touch with others, he is completely
controlled by others without knowing that he is; and
our view of him cancels the view that he simultaneously has of himself, so that he loses all cohesiveness
and becomes as it were transparent. And at the same
time his will is flouted, since his self-will is the
mother of his deafness, his blindness, and his downfall. A soundly constructed comedy is a regulation
hunt that has to end in the destruction of the quarry.
There is a comic awareness as there is a morbid
awareness. No one ever defined and stabilized it more
clearly than Molière did. Sganarelle is his first very
distinct outline of it. Let Molière bear down a little
harder, and the result will be Arnolphe; a little harder
still, and it will be Alceste.

Molière, in the midst of his triumph with L'École
des Maris, found himself compelled to undertake a
feat of sorts. The comptroller, Fouquet, was to entertain the king in his château at Vaux. He had to have
a comedy ready for August 17. Molière went to work
on it at once. It was incumbent on him not to miss
the smallest fraction of the opportunities that turned
up, especially opportunities of this sort. Under pressure he had one of those ideas that come to a man
hard pressed. He would usher on to the stage one
after another of the folk known as bores—folk who
do nothing themselves, but turn up as stumbling blocks
in the path of those who have no time to waste. Thus
he spared himself the invention of a plot and came

down to a single comic motif—one as various within its monotony, however, as an Arabian melody; a nightmare, too, of the sort in which one's progress is time after time interrupted by phantoms. And the nightmare is Molière's own.

One ingenious biographer has fancied that *Les Fâcheux* rehearses Molière's vexation on being prevented by intruders from going to Armande—a far-fetched guess that misses the perfectly obvious symbolism of the play. Time is incalculably valuable to Molière. His days are like soldiers' packs, with too little room for too many things. A man so harassed, with the temperament that we know was native to Molière, does not tamely put up with any part of life that is not sheer necessity. Whatever is added to necessity exasperates him, especially when it means the obliging bestowal of favors on persons wrapped up in themselves; for nothing so maddens the hard-pressed good workman as those who do not even notice that he is in a hurry. He is impatient, but he is powerless; and their gestures and wheedling speeches, made noxious by their utter pointlessness, are underlined and distorted by his controlled impatience. It is this that explains the halo worn by the portraits in Molière's gallery and missing from La Bruyère's. Eraste in his encounters with Orphise, Lysandre, Caritidès, and the others is a minor and more trivial version of Molière in collision with all the originals after whom he modeled his comic protagonists. For the comic character in Molière is made up of the superfluous attributes that turn him into a bore for the person with insistent interests and feelings to satisfy. Here is the origin of the repressed impatience that we call reason or nature; it seems to me to be a life-or-death need for simplification. But any such idea of what is superfluous depends on one's idea of what is necessary; and on that point the difference of opinion between Molière and many great minds will never be resolved.

This comedy-to-order was planned to supply the excuse for a ballet in which Fouquet could display a lavishness worthy of his celebration. Molière, in collaboration with LeBrun and with the stage manager, Torelli, had the idea of interpolating the dance figures into the play as entr'actes. These figures themselves constituted part of the plot of *Les Fâcheux*—an innovation from which Molière was later to derive some noteworthy effects. This contrivance was planned to make the most of the small available number of good dancers without letting the audience lose the thread of the comedy. Before the curtain rose Molière "appeared on-stage in ordinary clothes and, addressing the king with the countenance of someone taken by surprise, apologized for the confusion in which he was caught there all by himself, without the time or the players to provide His Majesty with the entertainment he seemed to be expecting. Simultaneously, in the midst of twenty jets of water from fountains, there opened wide that shell which everyone has seen, and the lovely naiad who was revealed in it came forward to the edge of the stage and in epic strain delivered the lines that Monsieur Pellisson had composed by way of prologue."

When Molière had spoken La Fontaine went on with the distinguished recital:

. . . By towering firs and in a lace of watery jets,
    Surrounded by the gracious coolth
Of fountains, forest, woodland shade, and wafts of air,
    The choice delights that we shall share
    Have been made ready for tonight.
With bosky leafage you shall find our stage bedight
    And fivescore torches set alight
To make the heavens envious. And, pray you, know,
    When part these curtains, everything—
Our music, fountains, lights, the stars, and all at Vaux—
Shall vie together for the joyance of the king. . . .

"In that prologue la Béjart, representing the nymph of the fountains where the action takes place, com-

manded her subordinate divinities to come forth from
the enclosing marble and do all that in them lay for
the delectation of His Majesty; and thereupon the
busts and statues that make part of the decoration of
the theater came to life, and from them came forth—
but how I know not—the fauns and bacchantes that
perform one of the figures of the ballet. And a droll
enough sight it is, this seeing a mere bust on a pedestal
brought to bed and its offspring dancing the moment
it comes into the world. All this takes place within
the comedy, which has to do with a man detained by
all manner of folk on his way to the keeping of a love
tryst."

> Molière it was that made this play—
> A writer who has found the way
> To ravish one and all at court.
> His name is of so fair report
> He must have hailed from Italy.
> I'm for him; he's the man for me.
> Bethink you, quite a while ago
> The knowing ones had come to know
> That he would surely make at home
> In France all Terence gave to Rome.
> Plautus, say you? A clownish bore!
> It never was so good before
> The cup of comedy to quaff.
> For there is none today to laugh
> At many a jape, now long passé,
> That served *in illo tempore*.
> We do these things in new-found ways,
> Have no more use for Jodelets,
> And think it now theatric sin
> Not to fit Nature like her skin.

The king was present at the spectacle, and with him
the queen mother, Monsieur, Monsieur's wife, and a
good part of the court. They had come from Fontainebleau by carriage, with the exception of Monsieur's wife, who had been borne in a litter. Louis
XIV took delight in this retinue of self-centered
crotcheteers, these simulacra of folly and idleness. As
a man not inimical to the truth he approved the

accuracy of the delineations. As a lover of spectacles he commended the marvels devised for his delight. After the ballet he congratulated Molière and also brought it to his attention that one noteworthy bore was missing from his constellation: Monsieur de Soyecourt, who belabored everybody with his hunting stories. The king was thereby giving Molière not only his own collaboration, but also the handsomest demonstration of real interest. Molière quickly got up the vocabulary of the chase—according to some, with the coaching of Monsieur de Soyecourt himself, which would have been a gracious enough concession. When, a few days later, the company enacted *Les Fâcheux* before the queen, who had been kept at Fontainebleau by her pregnancy, Molière played the hunter's scene in a scarlet jerkin, buckskin gloves, and yellow canvas boots.

Les Fâcheux was the first of Molière's plays to be dedicated to the king. On a stage that was symbolical in more than one way, there in the grounds at Vaux, with the fireworks drawing to a close, we have our first glimpse of Louis XIV and Molière side by side. The interest that the king had taken in the art of comedy—an interest dating from the time when, standing up and leaning on Mazarin's chair, he had watched an example of it—was doubtless mixed up with various other motives, but entirely to Molière's benefit. We know with what thoughtful steadfastness, and also with what a sense of stagecraft, Louis XIV played his part. The doctrine of divine right, which was as rabidly asserted then as the democratic or the proletarian ideal is today, provided him with all the religion he needed for a whole-souled belief in his mission—there is no doubting that; but his religion was given shape by a theatrical conception, or rather a conception of the theater. To this trait, add a very keen appetite for reasonableness that affiliated him with the middle class, not only in his methods, but also in his feeling. Molière, in his own province, was the perfect exemplar of what Louis XIV expected of those who served him. He was a wonderful deviser of entertainments and a wonderful observer of human behavior. The earnest turn taken by his criticism of life pleased the king's earnest mind; his comedies could play a part in the reorganization of France that was to begin with the fall from favor of their excessively ostentatious late host. Also, Molière was a middle-class man, neither more nor less so than Colbert; astray in a dubious sort of background, to be sure, but the more dependent on the king for that reason. In fine, he was a clown, but subject to a sovereign to whom it was a matter of course to elevate his clown to the dignity of Secretary of State for Ridicule.

As for Molière, his feeling about the king is sufficiently manifest. He was overjoyed to have pleased Louis XIV a little more unmistakably and to have got a little closer to him. The king was everything to Molière—his lord, his refuge, his cornerstone, his ace of trumps. Molière's love for the king was love for a permitted and promised success; it was the gratification of being able to give free rein to his energy. For to the tense and ambitious Frenchmen of that time, ranging all the way from Colbert to Molière, freedom meant a status that had constantly to be reconquered; and the king was their country in an embodiment that could be talked to. Molière must have been but little affected by the downfall of Fouquet, which coincided with his own rise in Louis XIV's favor. Fouquet constituted an independent light-giving center not to be tolerated in the new system of political astronomy. Molière, in no sense one of his parasites, had only to take his weapons, accouterments, scenery, actors, and genius and put them at the disposal of the one master who would thenceforth have the right to afford any supremely lavish festivals. The performances at Vaux and at Fontainebleau had brought in 15,428 livres. A lover of fiction would discover all manner of suggestive parallels at this point. Molière's career coincides with the most forthright, fruitful, and stable section of Louis XIV's reign. It was about 1672 that the budgetary balance established by Colbert was finally upset. Nevertheless all those thousands of livres soon to pile up were already harassing the comptroller general's too short nights. The harmony of a harmonious reign turns out to be pretty jangling if you listen intently. What was sheer necessity to Molière would become to Colbert an abominable superfluity.

Molière's marriage contract was signed January 23, 1662. The religious ceremony was performed at Saint Germain l'Auxerrois on February 28. By special dispensation of the vicar general of Paris the banns were pronounced but once. Before the marriage both Molière and Madeleine had been living at the intersection of the Rue Saint Thomas du Louvre and the Rue Saint Honoré, in a house in which the Molière-Béjarts, the de Bries, and the du Parcs divided living quarters. Molière was now to settle himself and his bride in the Rue de Richelieu, thereby evading— though, as we shall see, not for long—the involved promiscuities that seem an integral part of his fate. Utter silence surrounds those earliest hours of his wedded life. They have been dealt with; they will be dealt with exhaustively; but nothing will ever be known about them.

Molière did not stop working and could hardly have done so, but for some time he wrote nothing new. After Lent, at the beginning of the new theater season, Brécourt and Captain La Thorillère shifted from the Marais to the Palais Royal. Armande was officially enrolled in the company. Meanwhile the Italians reappeared in Paris. They paid Monsieur's players 2000 livres for the use of their auditorium, and this time it was they who had to be satisfied with the off days. The troupe from the provinces had really got somewhere in four years. In this year, 1662, Molière's company would appear to have been decidedly the one favored by the court and the grandees. Its "guest appearances" greatly increased in number. Several times it put on command performances at

Saint Germain en Laye, where Louis XIV was spending the vacation season; and it was paid on a princely scale. All this went on quite without reference to the Grands Comédiens; the time when they were being asked to pass judgment on the scared invaders from the provinces was now long gone. La Grange tells us that the queen mother "summoned the Hôtel de Bourgogne actors, who besought her to obtain for them the benefit of serving the king, they being extremely jealous of Molière's troupe." But Anne of Austria was of the elder generation, a world away. Racine had not yet made his advent to bring back to the Hôtel de Bourgogne its former prestige. By December 26, when *L'École des Femmes* was performed, the feud was fully developed, and a lesser triumph would have made it burst into overt hostilities.

The biographer of Molière confronts at this point the extremely intricate problem whether *L'École des Femmes* is in part autobiographical. The difficulty arises mostly, I think, from putting the question in the wrong terms. We ransack the *story* in the play for parallels to Molière's marital life. Since we have only the sketchiest information about his marital life, we can draw on nothing but the play itself and a handful of pamphlets to establish the resemblance. But those who refuse to detect any intimate disclosures in this fine work do not reason much more persuasively. Their chief argument is that Molière, by depicting himself in the guise of Arnolphe and making capital of the approximate difference in age between Armande and himself, was very injudiciously compromising his own interests. Their assumption is, then, that Molière would not have delved into his own private life except for practical considerations—that his choice was dictated by mere convenience. This assumption overlooks his being a poet. A poet may very well embody one side of himself in a work, and that unwittingly, without thereby making himself "like" his subject matter, which will be prescribed by any number of different considerations; he may do so, for example, by probing the implications of a difference in age between his wife and himself or by giving free rein to proclivities of his own that in private life he represses. The point has been stressed that such a girl as Armande, brought up in a rabble of stage folk, could not have much likeness to the pure Agnès. But here we have more hairsplitting over the word "likeness." By assuming as true a possibility of which we know nothing whatever, we could make the following surmise: Molière discovers that his wife does not return his love, persuades himself that her frigidity has no connection at all with any evil propensities, and extenuates her deficiency, exonerating her of every vestige of depravity and showing that with a person so innately virginal one is helpless. Or, conversely, Molière, being happily married and completely trusting his wife, rids himself of a tyrannical and jealous disposition lest it wreck his marriage. And it may be that Molière was both of these men, successively or even simultaneously. The theories for and against any specific autobiographical content in *L'École des Femmes* are but imaginings. But to say that is far from saying that there is nothing in common between Arnolphe and Molière.

We marvel at Molière's genius, his assimilation of experience; we hold as an article of faith that the cardinal attributes of a creative writer work together as if apart from himself. But what we have here is the confrontation of a man with a woman on a stage. The crucial point is not that Arnolphe is old enough to be Agnès's father: it is that he brought her up, or at least fell into a paternal way of treating her, and that now it is otherwise than as a father that he wants her to love him. The subtle point is not a young girl's acceptance of an older man as her husband, but the conversion before her very eyes of a father man into a husband man while she herself is unable to transform her behavior and attitude. Léonor's feeling in *L'École*

des Maris is a filial one. Agnès's situation is more delicate and also more desperate. She can give Arnolphe
the love due to a father, but she cannot endure him
as her husband, and ill fortune decrees that Arnolphe
shall instinctively resort to the father's authority to
impose himself on her as a husband. The clash of
these two attitudes and the shuttling back and forth
between them make the comic core of *L'École des
Femmes*. So far from being the story of a lover too
far advanced in years, the play is the drama of a man
too young for the task he has undertaken.

Molière lays bare to our sight the play of blind
impulses that underlies all the theories about the will
and all its ridiculous gestures. He lays bare the force
that actuates people—the force that governs the unfolding of a life as it governs the unfolding of a play.
Arnolphe's natural energy is self-defeating, because it
undertakes to act on another energy, not reckoning
with what that other energy is—a miscalculation of
the laws of mechanics. Arnolphe, who is pure instinct, becomes in relation to Agnès pure will; that is,
pure nullity. That is the source of his tragedy and the
source of our laughter. Agnès's inherent nature prevails over his because it remains self-sufficient. All
Arnolphe's quaverings, his foamings and seethings, are
futile. All the self-improvement that he carries out in
order to "sell" himself is communicated to Agnès, but
without Arnolphe himself. Marriage and its jars she
can face; but why with him? Completion of the
circle is inevitable. When at last Arnolphe gives up,
when he is brought abjectly to his knees, when we see
him utterly defenseless before Agnès, what wretched-
ness there is, and what an impassable gulf, between
these two beings chained to each other! Helplessness
to "put oneself across" in an argument or an outburst
is one of the signal experiences that we find anato-
mized in this masterpiece.

And the helplessness of the will is another. The line
from *Sertorius* that Arnolphe quotes has a symbolical
force. Neither Descartes nor Corneille would have

conceded that victory of the mechanical. Bergson's famous theory is hardly applicable to *L'École des Femmes* or to Molière's profound humanity in general; or rather you can hardly apply it save by inverting it. The automatism here is the closest possible approximation of life itself, and it is this very automatism that our laughter reveals to us when it dispels the illusion of will power. Agnès's voice is the voice of a medium. So we read the deeper meaning of *L'École des Femmes*. Wiped out are the delusions of authority, the romantic creator, the will as architect of happiness; they have given way to natural laws, impulsiveness, mechanical toys whose machinery works smoothly together, toys that wreck each other when they collide—a human machinery that flouts all the more exalted forms of authority along with all its lowlier forms. But what, among such realities, is to be the place of passion, of impulse seeking its release, of the self driven by need of other selves?

It is a struggle for a man to make terms with this world new to himself, new to the vast majority of his fellows, perhaps new to Molière himself. Between Sganarelle and Arnolphe there is a conspicuous progression. Sganarelle was without awareness of his situation. Arnolphe, by a significant reversal, finds his eyes suddenly opened. He ushers in a new breed of comic protagonist, the man whom neither his awareness nor his will power can deliver from the situation that is making him comic. We are already well on the way to Alceste. Sganarelle has no love for Isabelle. When he finds that he has been deceived he gives up forthwith and takes himself off—

> That lying sex forever I forswear;
> The devil seize the lot for all I care.

Compare this utterance with that of Agnès's lord and master:

> A curious business, love—on those deceivers
> To waste such weaknesses, such fears and fevers!
> Their foibles are an open book to all:

The sex, extravagant and whimsical,
With mind erratic, disposition vicious,
Is everything most silly and capricious,
Faithless to boot. And, blind to all such features,
We tear ourselves to bits to serve the creatures.

Thus, our laughter is wrung out of the pangs suffered by Arnolphe—pangs that are completely human and completely dramatic. Remember the well-known uncompleted "the—" with which he signalizes an occasion of intense jealousy, reflected like everything in Molière by the graphic quality of the dialogue. And yet he continues to be comic, by reason of the contradiction between his determination and his mischances; by reason of his contempt for ordinary opinion; by reason of his gift for taking his place among the very sort of persons who elicit his gibes. Molière was never to achieve a more brilliant success in the precise telescoping of two levels of consciousness—the comic consciousness of the audience and the dramatic or tragic consciousness of the actor; the drama that, as it completely unfolds, conveys to us as it lists and with all its power the laughter that releases us from its spell and the discernment that passes sentence on it. Molière has solved the insoluble problem. Comic and tragic are united, fused together; it is comedy that profits, yet tragedy loses not an iota of its prerogative as an expression of reality. Nothing could be more comic than *L'École des Femmes*, yet nothing could be more inexorable or more singly dedicated to inexorableness. Such is the human experience embodied in this comedy. Draw from it what autobiographic inferences you will, but if you consider it as incorporating truths that are apparently to be arrived at only by the route of self-conquest, you will find it difficult to divorce this experience from the most intimate feelings of Molière himself.

If *L'École des Femmes* was not the greatest triumph in the history of the seventeenth-century theater, it was one of the greatest. The first eleven performances brought in 12,747 livres. Enacted thirty-one times before Easter, the play was resumed after the Easter holidays, still to packed houses. Persons able to afford "guest performances" arranged private showings for themselves. To crown all, the king took delight in the play. For a number of months Molière, thanks to the sensation of his triumph and the sensation of the royal favor—which intensified the attacks of which he was the target—had the literary spotlight all to himself. The man who had been dealt with hitherto as a buffoon shot with luck had suddenly acquired a disconcerting importance. His licenses and coarsenesses to the contrary notwithstanding, there he was, cutting a figure as a poet and, as if under cover of one desperate assault, thrusting comedy into a position to outrage everything that was being admired in serious drama. *L'École des Femmes* contains an undefined element of strain, contrivance, overstatement —in a word, inflation—that is not proof against invidious criticism. All this clearly arises out of the farcical element, without quite achieving independence of it; so that one is justified in detecting in it a kind of chicanery. Mere malice does not account for the indignation of Molière's enemies. The hierarchy of literary forms had been disrupted. All the folk that were hanging around the threshold of the temple of good taste, as the poor hang around that of a church, found themselves driven out. Now that the sovereignty of the sublime had been challenged, those who were profiting by its rituals were suddenly jobless. There is no such thing as giving people an illusion of laughter; to laugh is a bodily jolt and a social transaction, and either you do or you don't. If it had become necessary, in order to achieve repute, to venture on a frightful test that one had hitherto had every right to scorn, would it not be preferable first to try every possible means of restoring the traditional order of values?

It is to be added that the success of *L'École des Femmes* coincided with a revolution in the system of patronage in France. Literature was by no means

exempt from the general centralizing policy of Louis
XIV. There was now a single overlord, a single
patron, a single object of tribute. The same will was
behind the building of ships of the line and the composition of eulogies. Colbert made Chapelain, Per-
rault, and several others responsible for directing the
glorification of the king. At Easter they made public
a preliminary list of annual allowances. In it Molière
was down for a thousand livres, and he was characterized as a first-rank comic poet. This list has been
called an absurdity, and some have cried out against
finding Molière less well rewarded in it than certain
negligible historians. Contemporaries saw the matter
in a quite different light, and rightly. Allowances in
1663 were based not on the comparative merits of
works—merits hard enough to prove, anyway—but
on the social importance of different classes of works.
Now that the whole wealth of France was going into
the royal coffers and living quarters, applicants for
favors were encountering one another at the same
doorway. These allowances being annual, their re-
newal had to be earned every year—an encouragement to treacheries and double-dealings, which are
among the most automatic devices of competition.

A young fellow of twenty-five, by name Visé, out-
lined the campaign well before Easter, about the end
of February, in his *Nouvelles Nouvelles*. His way of
going about it is informative. He is wary; he sets
down the pros and the contras; he makes himself a
sounding board for the various estimates that the
comedy has evoked. He feels strongly that the last
word has not been said and that there is still time left
for attacking Molière; his primary purpose is to
advertise himself without being too deeply committed.
Molière's rejoinders were shortly to ruffle this equanimity. Throughout the controversy over *L'École des
Femmes* Molière was to achieve a nice combination
of discretion with boldness. He let his opponents have
the floor first, his *Critique de l'École des Femmes*

being the first public exhibition of the attacks on
him; for Visé's criticisms can hardly figure as a
declaration of war. By this tactic Molière compelled his adversaries to accept, willy-nilly, the characterization of themselves that he thrust upon them.
At the same time he took pains to lay down a fair-
and-square definition of his claims, asserting them the
while as rights. Also he took advantage of the situation to set up an implied covenant between the king
and himself—a kind of reciprocal undertaking that
the king was to reap enjoyment and Molière himself
patronage. This implication is distinctly perceptible
in his *Remerciement au Roi*. He costumes his muse as
a marquis for his call to thank the king for the allowance he has just received, and he makes it the
occasion for an irresistible take-off of a courtier at
the Louvre. Molière had inherited his brother's com-
mission as upholsterer *valet de chambre*, and that
status ushers him into the intimacy of the court and
allows him to exchange with Louis XIV some respect-
fully informal scraps of conversation, broken off just
short of becoming permissions or commands and
capable of turning into either as required. Louis XIV
was doubtless not irked by letting Molière serve as
the court's disciplinary officer, and when Molière
declares to us that henceforth every valet in comedy
is going to be replaced by a marquis, his boldness is
unquestionably countenanced on the king's part.
On June 2, 1663 he put on a performance of a
fresh divertissement that he had advertised in his
preface to *L'École des Femmes*—a comedy in conversation in which the critics of his great comedy
were introduced and discussed. In it Molière exhibits
himself as a skillful winnower of public opinion. All
in turn get their comeuppance—the impotent high
priests of the Accepted Way, the précieuses who have
overstayed their time, the witless marquis, the sham
highbrows who embrace court and pit in one identical
condescension. All these folk are made to seem, in

the *Critique*, not so much silly as behind the times.
Molière is unapproached in his knack of making opponents look obsolete.

But he had other concerns, too, and more momentous ones. He delivered the brunt of his attack against
those who would deny to comedy its title to equal
rank with the "serious" drama. In pursuance of a
going concern—possibly, too, with a more or less
unfocused realization of his own aesthetic development—Molière aimed his shaft over the heads of his
detractors at Corneille himself. The technique of his
self-defense is particularly striking. He does not ac-
cuse tragedy of being too solemn; he has too much
dexterity to fall into that trap. He accuses it of being
too *easy*. It is child's play to imagine things, but fear-
fully difficult to observe them truly, and "it is an
unearthly undertaking, this making respectable folk
laugh." Here we have an assertion that sublimity of
Corneille's kind is but fantasy. Today we should put it
that the seamy side of the heroic is truer than the
glorious side. This attitude speaks volumes about
Molière's self-sublimations in the serious drama. In the
interest of making Don Garcie overconsistent with
"nature" he had dedicated him, under protest, to
laughter. But the direct thrust at Corneille is no mere
by-product of a personal apologia. For the comic to
become poetic, reality and some sort of ideal must
come face to face and demonstrate their incompatibility—a confrontation that takes place only at some
special junctures of history. When it does take place
the comic dual vision really achieves its full human
import.

Molière had vindicated his art in his *Critique* by the
success of *L'École des Femmes*—an entirely rational
piece of pragmatism, for he meant, not that the only
rule is to be amusing, but that the audience's amusement signifies that the important rules have been applied. His opponents supplied a signal corroboration
by resorting to his own style, his own characters, and

his own devices in order to confute him. Boursault, in his *Portrait du Peintre*, staged at the Hôtel de Bourgogne in early October, is satisfied merely to "turn the coat inside out." The play misses fire as an avowed criticism of the *Critique*, but the fact remains that it borrows its diction from Molière. Boursault had been recognized in the figure of Lysandre in the *Critique*, or rather he had seen fit to recognize himself. Like Visé, he was youthful, ambitious, and possibly backed by more influential persons. Molière was present at the performance. Regardless of the mediocrity of the play, he thought it expedient to reply to it: it contained innuendoes that he neither would nor could ignore.

His enemies, goaded and somewhat dazed by his onset, unmasked all their batteries at once. Corneille with his overt resentment, and his brother Thomas with his obvious malevolence, gave warrant for the affecting references to their quondam greatness. But that was not enough. The earliest references to Molière's irreligion and to his marital misfortunes were already turning up in the pamphlets that appeared one after another and in the lobby of the Palais. Persons who still had only a very limited comprehension of the sort of favor Molière enjoyed tried to stir up the nobility against him. Strange rumors circulated about him. In one scene of the *Critique* the marquis who is hostile to Molière, when called on to state why he thinks the famous "cream tart" passage so bad, makes himself a laughingstock by reiterating "cream tart" without managing to formulate a vestige of critical opinion. It was being whispered about that the Duc de la Feuillade had actually said the words that Molière had transferred to the stage. A few days after the *Critique* was performed this same Duc de la Feuillade, encountering Molière in the king's waiting room, was supposed to have made the beckoning gesture of a man who has something to say to another. Molière approached him and bowed, whereupon the nobleman seized Moliére's head with both hands and ground it against his coat buttons, yelling "Cream tart, Molière, cream tart!" A Molière with his periwig askew and his face streaming blood, slinking off through the passageways of the Louvre; an infidel Molière taking advantage of his misdirected popularity to inject all manner of poison into the minds of his audience; a mountebank who has got himself into the Temple of Taste by simple burglary—such is the specimen that was beginning to take shape. Something had to be done about it.

Molière did something about it instanter, and with his uncanny artfulness. His pretext—imaginary—should be an urgent order from the king for a new comedy, one that he had to leave unfinished for lack of time. The play should represent a series of sketchy rehearsals, with the actors' discussions interlarded; and inasmuch as these actors should be impersonating themselves under their actual names, Molière in his own person should be able to answer his enemies from the stage instead of by the roundabout route of an imagined character. It was just a week after *Portrait du Peintre* that *L'Impromptu de Versailles* was acted, to the applause of the whole court. It spoke an unmistakable language and a telling one. Success, cited as the actual and only cause of the dispute, delivered the most devastating of retorts in the guise of a judicial restraint. Molière, patently emboldened by the royal authorization, dropped his mask and held forth with a rigidly controlled solemnity:

"I surrender ungrudgingly to them my works, my carriage, my gestures, my words, my intonation, and my manner of delivery, that they may make of them and say of them whatsoever they please, if they are able to get any good out of them. To all this I offer not the slightest resistance, and I shall rejoice that such things can afford people pleasure. But when I surrender all this to them, they should do me the kindness to leave me the residue. They should let severely alone every matter of the order of those for which, I am told, they assail me in their comic plays. For this boon I courteously beseech that cultivated gentleman who lends them a hand with their writings. And that is the last word that I have to say to them."

Nevertheless Molière had never been at a loss for a way to press his advantages. He seized the occasion to deliver a home thrust at the actors of the Hôtel de Bourgogne, his enemies' base of operations. He attacked them with the weapon that he wielded so consummately: he mimicked them—and, as all men know, adroit mimicry is at once the least answerable and the most unendurable of affronts.

The countercharge from the Hôtel de Bourgogne was not long in arriving. First there came *La Vengeance des Marquis*, by Visé—this time an enraged Visé; then, in December, *L'Impromptu de l'Hôtel de Condé*, by the younger Montfleury. About the same time the elder Montfleury put before the king the charming petition that Racine recorded for us. Visé had had printed, simultaneously with his play, a *Lettre sur les Affaires du Théâtre*, and a man named Robinet had followed suit with a *Panégyrique de l'École des Femmes*—a delusive title. We may mention in addition *Les Amours de Calotin*, by Chevalier, acted at the beginning of 1664—it bears witness to Molière's overwhelming success—and, finally, *La Guerre Comique*, by Philippe de la Croix. Molière simply held his peace. He was honoring the promise he had made to himself in *L'Impromptu de Versailles*.

Of all those pamphlets flung out like a shower of pebbles there is now almost nothing left. It is poetic justice that there should survive one diverting scene from *La Vengeance des Marquis* (which may well have inspired the Marivaux of *L'Île des Esclaves*) in which we see a manservant taking Molière literally and setting out to dress his master as a valet of the comic stage. In all objectiveness, and possibly with some reluctance, we have to grant that Molière triumphed all along the line. The *Critique* and the *Impromptu* are something a great deal better than occasional plays. Each is a model in its kind. Still and all, one would like to cheer for a fine sally or two from the other side of the barricade. Molière, as the cumulative effect of defending himself and doing it too well, ends by exasperating us. He is too well supported, too sure of himself, too sure of the king. The Grands Comédiens, when all is said, were not merely ridiculous; Racine was soon to make himself responsible for teaching Molière thus much, or for reminding him of it. What was now in short supply was poetic talent. Caught unaware, poorly equipped, this company was doing its best. In any event it was no fault of Molière's that its poor best was not better.

What did he get out of this war over comedy? What were his gains from it, and what his losses? The gains heavily preponderated. Over and above the assured support of Louis XIV and the exquisite delight of giving delight to the king, Molière won from the struggle, to begin with, the one consummation for which he the most deeply cared: the elevation of comedy to the topmost rank of literary forms. Thus much is attested by the stanzas Boileau wrote—beguiling lines surcharged with an aroma of classic antiquity rejuvenated. And do not fail to note that this success was devoid of all connection with what Molière's adversaries called high comedy. It had to do solely with the form originated by Molière, in which farce imparted its heightening effect to ideas, and which at one bound attained identity with the universal comic form. Molière, with a dexterity that has been insufficiently acclaimed, made profitable use of the criticisms while going through the motions of confuting them. Publicly he vindicated the impudicities of his play: privately he resolved to make his major comedies more and more suitable for decorous folk. In them we miss the amazing and complex flavor of *L'École des Femmes*, but the prestige of the type is enhanced.

He accomplishes still more. In the *Critique* he has his mouthpiece Dorante say: "And as to the amorous frenzy of Act V, which they criticize as being too overdrawn and too ludicrous, I should just like to know if that is not the way to make fun of lovers; also if respectable folk, even the gravest of them, in like situations do not do things— In short, if we were to take one good look at ourselves when we are really enamored—" The generalization gets buried under the marquis's jeers, but what Moliére is driving at does not elude us. If the most serious-minded, if we ourselves "when we are really enamored," might enact the comedy that is Arnolphe's, then ridicule is no treatment reserved for a few exceptional characters outside the pale of seemly society; then ridicule is an outlook upon all mankind, a technique for arresting ourselves and for arresting others at any stage whatever of intimacy or of deep involvement. In other words it is a mode of expression that is viable, on the same terms as tragedy, for every human reality that is to be expressed. Molière is not satisfied to engraft comedy upon serious drama: his aspiration is nothing less than to broaden the form and firmly to entrench comedy in a position side by side with tragedy. Comedy must be serious in meaning in the degree that it is humorous in process. It was about 1664 that Molière weeded out of his repertoire all the little potboiling farces—"the time at which," La Grange tells us, "he adopted as the aim of all his plays that they should compel people to mend their shortcomings."

But the war over comedy partly balanced its gains with losses, too. Molière was tired, and he was going to be more and more tired, inescapably. The incessant struggle and tension; the compulsion to be vigilant from morning to night; the strain of being constantly amusing, no less toilsome than the strain of self-defense; the management of his troupe, his playhouse, his profession, his creative ideas; the innuendoes and slanders that left their deposits in public opinion— deposits that no royal edict could sweep into limbo;

finally, the obscure marital difficulties that, whatever their cause, are only too unquestionable as facts—these exactions left Molière as little freedom from harassment as any man of genius ever had. But the very forces that made the man waste away made the man's calling flourish. From all that extracts the vitality from him he extracts an ever more resourceful inventiveness, an ever more majestic audacity.

THE GAMESTER IN COMEDY

Molière was forty-two. He was fairly tall, rather stocky of build, though agile. His hair and his eyes were jet black. The middle part of his face was long in proportion to its lower part. The wide spacing of his eyes and a faint suggestion of the negroid in his lips and at the base of his nose accounted for the attractiveness of features that curiously combined coarseness and fineness. His expression was of the earth, earthy; his glance fleet, eager, and given to dwelling on people. His pace was deliberate. At court, or when he was out walking, or in places of business, or behind the scenes, his countenance would be seen as immobile, not to say frozen. But this same countenance would instantaneously unfreeze; its features would twist, lose composition, quickly regain it—a visage of flexible masks of flesh that emerged one from another at will. Then the face would regain its impassiveness and become again withdrawn. He could tell his sedate body to make faces, too. He had trained it to muscular flexions that emphasized its contours and in a few simple motions sketched the vignette of a weakness or a vice. That kind of mastery over bodily signals has its echo in the brain and colors the mental processes: when Molière was writing he was also mimicking, and the words must have shaped themselves in his facial creases and in his whole frame. Yet this flexibility did not produce the smallest abatement in a kind of rigidity that we consistently sense in him—a rigidity of instinct that would neither break nor bend, a rigidity of judgment that passed instantaneous verdicts. Before everything he was alive. He excited, goaded, restrained, pre-empted. He was one of the least absent-minded men that ever lived.

Molière was susceptible to some degree of ostentation—to a lavish definition of living. His company now had two shares of the profits earmarked for him, besides his wife's share; before long he was to have five. The money that he earned restored the middle-class dignity that he had forgone. He bought fine furniture and fine clothes; he was fond of sumptuous and solid belongings. He indulged himself, then, in his brief sojourns and fleeting respites; for he lacked the time for leisurely enjoyment. His career is like that of the acrobat who has to practice all day lest he kill himself in the evening. We have to take into account, too, the everyday vexations of theater life; we should be hard put to it to conceive what they were then. The relation between actors and public was subject to a rowdy, bullying familiarity that necessitated constant alertness and actual physical courage on the part of troupe managers. The troopers and the pages of the royal establishment did not mean to pay admission, and they would assault the watchmen and the unhappy doorkeeper; on one occasion the injuries inflicted cost the theater treasury fifty-five livres. With the doorkeeper knocked out and the watchmen beaten up, the roisterers would pour into the auditorium, and then there was an unending uproar. Between the rowdyism of the pit and the members of the aristocracy seated on the stage and cramping the actors' mobility, the spokesman of the troupe was under constant compulsion to devise stratagems, plead, banter, threaten, and cajole with timely sallies. Molière, besides performing this function, also had the task of announcing, before the last curtain, what the next day's show was to be. All told, there was enough to tire both body and brain.

Molière was taciturn. After such a freshet of words-to-order he would retreat into silence as if it were his birthright. His doing so denoted weariness as much as native inclination, no doubt; he had no strength to squander. And he was silent the better to observe. The incessant gabbler, the man who is always deflecting attention toward himself, does not remember very well. The age is sown with anecdotal glimpses of

Molière in the posture of wordless listener. He is extolled for his gravity, too; the "Molière who is no laugher" makes a pointed contrast with "Molière, God of Laughter." He clowned it on the stage; in privacy he was the man of good counsel—a grave, deliberate, somber man. It is not out of the question that he deliberately forged this sober personality when he made up his mind to raise comedy to the heights. So pliant a mimetic talent could have contrived as much without any great struggle; without any self-falsification, too, for if people need the guidance of conventional symbols, a sense of humor and a virtuosity in bearing and gesture are excellent teammates for sobriety of mind. Molière did not invest his entire moral capital in comedy for the sole reason that he had had but ill success in the tragic mode. In the very period when he was perfecting his art he was discovering that comic insight is a means of representing life in its entirety and that it can be congruous with any situation at all. Inasmuch as comic insight is dual, in him who evokes it from the most intimate and the most vital conflicts it presupposes a reflective detachment steadily maintained—a sense of truth and of illusion insistent enough to hold the field against the compromises of sentimentality. Despite his supposed regard for Descartes and Gassendi, the man whom Boileau styled the Man of Reflection, though a sound logician, was no philosopher. But a genius for comedy has in common with the genius for philosophy the requirement that it make the clearest possible distinction between what is thought and what is felt. The distinction calls for a vigorous and a flexible brain.

As for Molière's melancholy, we have next to no ground for questioning its actuality. No specific source states it as a fact, to be sure; but it would be decidedly astonishing if his contemporaries, friends and enemies alike, had unanimously conspired to give us a false picture. Grimarest preserves for us some actual or imagined remarks of Molière's that throw a clear light on his mood. When Chapelle expostulates

with him about his brooding tendency Molière re-
plies: "Oh, my dear fellow, you are certainly joking.
It is easy enough for you to follow your pattern of
living. You are shielded against everything. You can
put in a whole fortnight thinking up a pleasantry with
no one to bother you, and then, still well warmed
with wine, go and retail it everywhere at your friends'
expense. You haven't anything else to do. But if you
were busy, as I am, amusing the king, and if you had
to support and manage forty or fifty persons that
won't listen to reason, and a theater to keep going,
and works to compose to prop up your reputation,
you wouldn't want to laugh either—on my word you
wouldn't—and you wouldn't have anything like so
much attention to bestow on your fine wit. . . . If I
were looking for glory, my works would have quite a
different cast; but to support my company I have to
do my talking to a great motley of folk with very
few persons of wit among them, and those folk
wouldn't for a minute put up with your lofty style
and lofty sentiments. And when I've ventured on
something fairly tolerable, you've seen yourself how
hard put to it I was to wrest any scrap of success out
of it." "Shielded against everything": Molière himself
is no longer shielded against anything whatever, and
there, doubtless, is the key to his "brooding tendency." And we must understand that he is not even
shielded against himself. In the roving and detached
predicament of a Chapelle a man readily becomes
oblivious of his own burdens. What *L'École des
Femmes* reveals to us about Molière's experience—the
helplessness to bespeak his own happiness or to find in
others the feelings that he expects from them, to say
nothing of the obstacles he had encountered in getting
the importance of his message recognized—is surely
enough to dispirit a conscientious, sensitive, and extremely weary man. For we must always come back
to this weariness of his, which was soon to acquire a
more sinister name. The time was not remote when
disease, incipient bodily dissolution, would compel

Molière to abandon that stage to which he was bound
by so many debts of gratitude, so much depth of feeling, and such a load of cares.

In the opening months of 1664, nevertheless, Molière was on the verge of a five years' struggle beside
which the battle over *L'École des Femmes* was child's
play. From that struggle he was to wring both complete exhaustion and undying fame. When it was over
he would have won for comedy every prerogative to
which he was staking a claim; but it would appear
that, somewhat bewildered by his very boldness, he
was unable or disinclined to reap the fruits of his
triumph. *Tartuffe*, *Don Juan*, and *Le Misanthrope*
have been responsible for a wonderful shedding of
ink. After one has demolished all the gratuitous theories, after one has declined to ferret out any esoteric
meaning from these plays, one is still unable to take
exception to thus much: *Tartuffe* and *Don Juan* mean
that comedy knows no privileged vices, and *Le Misanthrope* means that comedy knows no privileged vir-
tues. Molière's contemporaries were not mistaken;
Rousseau was not mistaken; and it is this twofold
claim that matters—matters vastly more than Molière's
feelings about religion or his ideas about goodness. In
these plays it is not alone the literary pre-eminence of
comedy that Molière is striving to prove and to vindicate: it is also the privilege of the comic discernment to penetrate to the inmost recesses of personality. If we generalize from Dorante's words, we hear
Molière saying, or getting it said for him: "If we were
to take one good look at ourselves when we are really
pious—" and "If we were to take one good look at
ourselves when we are really concupiscent—" and "If
we were to take one good look at ourselves when we
are really virtuous—" But just when Molière's privilege of the one good look was challenged—at least so
far as piety and concupiscence were concerned—he
apparently perceived that the cool, amused reasonableness that validates comedy and constitutes its justification was put on the defensive by the freedoms

that his genius had won. Comic discernment was
being brought into conflict with comic propriety. Society had collaborated with Molière in his rise to
prestige: society would demand the restoration of its
own prerogatives and hale him back within its prescribed bounds. As we retrace the sudden turns of
fortune in the war over *Tartuffe* we must not forget
this other battle, the inner one, which involved Molière's profession and his whole being and completes
his intellectual portrait.

On January 19, 1664 Armande gave birth to Molière's first son, little Louis, who had the king and the
Duchesse d'Orléans for godparents. On January 29
the company played *Le Mariage Forcé* in the queen's
suite. This comedy ballet was then acted twice for
Madame (the Duchesse d'Orléans) and, beginning
February 15, twelve times at the Palais Royal. The
music was by Lully, the ballet by the president of the
council, de Périgny. A graceful and workmanlike
play in which Molière refines upon the style that he
had adumbrated in *Les Fâcheux*, it throws a valuable
light on Molière's mental processes in connection with
comedy. Indeed, the opening scene shows us how one
character *becomes* comic. Sganarelle becomes so at the
exact moment when his comrade, by way of demonstrating to him that he is too old to think of marrying,
would have him compute his age, and Sganarelle answers: "Oh, no, not that." What is an arithmetical
computation but the plainest, most rigorous language
of reason? Sganarelle's answer cuts him off from the
commonwealth of sensible minds. The reasoning faculty ceases to take the character seriously, and it is
with a merely objective awareness that we contemplate his woes. Asking a friend's advice and then forcing on him the advice that one was asking for—that is
the absolute paradigm of the comic relation between
the individual and other persons. When he puts more
trust in his own will to believe than in the facts of
arithmetic, when he exclaims "I tell you I have made
up my mind to get married," just as Alceste is later

to exclaim "I *will* get angry, and I *won't* listen," it needs no more to make the adviser or the friend take refuge in irony—and that is a species of absence-while-present that sunders more hopelessly than actual isolation. To take a person seriously is only to be at one with him; to take a person comedically is to be, so to speak, at two with him. And the protagonist becomes comic through his own determination, his own fiat, the insistence of his own blind egoism. George Dandin's "You asked for it!" denotes one of the integral requirements of comedy.

That Molière, in this occasional play, could draw with complete ease an accurate diagram of mental behavior means that he now had a very clear apprehension of the comic features that are part and parcel of the universal human face. Man becomes comic by virtue of a sort of madness, a derangement of the will; there are no feelings, no situations, that are inherently ridiculous as compared with others that are not. Tragic emotion and comic emotion can spring from causes of precisely the same category and with the same title to respect. The difference is in the outcome and in the organization of the work. Molière, anxious to advance himself while advancing the cause of comedy, was naturally impelled to choose targets for ridicule from among the most solemn, most important sentiments. The logic of his career and of his way of thinking decreed that he should do so.

For some time now—perhaps from late 1662—he had been revolving a plan that was both audacious and commensurate with his aspirations. Among the bores that irked self-respecting folk at the time, there were some of an exceedingly peculiar species. They did not badger people by dint of their egoism, in the way of an Arnolphe or a Lysandre or a Caritidès: they badgered people in God's name. The Society of the Holy Sacrament, founded in 1630 by the Duc de Ventadour, was a sodality for general Catholic propaganda. But it was a secret sodality. It did not limit itself to multiplying charities, weaving a provincial network

as the Jacobins were to do, manipulating bishops without their knowing it, and draping neckerchiefs over
prostitutes' bosoms: it wormed its way into family
secrets and aspired to correct personal morals *ad maio-
rem dei gloriam.* The founder had consecrated his
own wife to God, and an example of that sort served
as an excuse for anything. The members insinuated
themselves into private houses by devices "so bare-
faced and prying," as one priest said, "that they might
bring about a great deal of disturbance and family dis-
cord." In short, the religious devotee of tradition had
acquired a new celebrity, and the natural laws of ridicule dedicated him to the uses of high comedy.

He belonged, moreover, to an ambiguous class. A
miser, a middle-class climber, or an Arnolphe is know-
able, and he is homogeneous. An untimely devotee
that turns families upside down may be a scoundrel,
but he may also be a zealot. A Christian bigot is the
polar opposite of a scoundrel; but on a man of the
period a scoundrel and a zealot can produce exactly
the same impression and provoke the same righteous
wrath. The whole altercation over *Tartuffe* turns on
just this duplexity. The problem is not to determine
whether Molière did or did not believe in God: it is
to determine whether he was so far aloof from the
fervors of the Christian life as to be harassed, nettled,
and angered by religious excess; whether he was fond
enough of the mundane life to defend it with a kind
of patriotic ardor against the hatred that fanatical
Christians evinced for it. That he actually had this
aloofness and this patriotic ardor is scarcely open to
doubt. Nothing gives us any license to suppose that
Molière conceived *Tartuffe* by a process different
from the one that produced his other works.

In the king and in the wardens of the state he found
opinions in accord with his own. Louis XIV was, to
be sure, religious in an artless way, but he was young,
and Mademoiselle de La Vallière was about to present
him with a child. All he thought about was celebra-

tions and pompous displays. And the devotees an-
noyed him for some more serious reasons. It was a
matter of course for Louis XIV to consider himself on
friendly, not to say cosy, terms with the deity. He
surveyed those zealots pretty much as a great lord
surveys an ordinary citizen who tries to outdo him
in manners; that is to say, he found them unseemly.
And, finally, he was extremely well aware of himself
as the head of a great state that he meant to make still
greater. There was a radical, an intrinsic disparity between political progress and the great heavenward
drive that carried away so many souls set free from
earthly trammels. But there was no need to call attention to this disparity; doing so might sound a discordant note in the monarchical symphony. Molière sub-
mitted to the king his preliminary outline of *Tartuffe*,
or at the least sketched its plot for him. We have no
warrant for believing that, as has been asserted, *Tartuffe* was composed on instructions from Louis XIV;
but the king undoubtedly interposed no objections to
Molière. The Society of the Holy Sacrament got wind
of what was brewing and decided that it mattered. On
April 17 it decided to get the play suppressed. The
situation was complicated by the queen mother's ad-
vocacy at court of the devotees' cabal—the saintly
faction. The sequel is well known. The king pressed
Molière to stage his comedy at court at the first possible moment, just as it was, that he might gauge its
effect on his retinue (and perhaps on himself?). Or
did Molière himself decide to make due use of the
great Versailles festivities that were being organized
and in them to interpolate this dainty morsel? Certain
it is that those three acts of *Tartuffe* appeared on the
program of *Les Plaisirs de l'Île Enchantée*, between
Le Mariage Forcé and *Les Fâcheux*.

The occasion was in every way an ideal choice. It
was ostensibly in honor of the queens that Louis XIV
had ordered the festivities. They were mounted with
extraordinary pomp at Versailles at the beginning of

May 1664. Mademoiselle de La Vallière's lying-in had
gone off well, and everybody knew that this splendid
tribute was actually meant for her. In late April a
motley of folk had swooped down on Versailles—
handicraftsmen, messengers, actors, dancers, pyrotech-
nists, musicians, and all the king's household services.
When the courtiers got there, there was hardly any
room left, and the king did not bother his head about
finding them some. Nobles as important as de Guise
and d'Elbeuf "had hardly a hole to hide in." They had
to make shift with the cold comfort of marveling at
all the gold and marble that "vied with each other in
beauty and brilliance." The theaters were erected in
the grounds. The spectacle had been arranged in daily
units, with a shift of scene each day; the last day's
move took the spectators before the palace of Alcine,
where the transfiguration was to take place. Alcine
was a sorceress who was keeping in durance on her
enchanted island the traditional heroes of chivalry.

On the opening day a mighty wind sprang up, and
it lasted throughout the festivities, but the structures
withstood it, and no attention was paid to it. People
were altogether too busy marveling at the unlucky
but splendid knights, who were no lesser persons than
the king, the ducs of Saint Aignan, de Noailles, de
Guise, de Foix, and de Coaslen, the marquis d'Humi-
ères and de La Vallière, the Comte d'Armagnac, and
the Comte du Lude, all in the most regal costumes and
mounted on steeds wondrously caparisoned. An "in-
finity of lights" illumined the pageant and the repasts,
and each of these last "could rank as one of the most
sumptuous banquets possible to serve." Molière and his
company were collaborating with the most illustrious
personages in France. Mademoiselle du Parc, in a
green robe adorned with silver and real flowers, impersonated Spring, mounted on a Spanish horse.
"Along with the sex and the charms of a woman she
showed a man's dexterity." La Grange, as Apollo,
addressed some disingenuous compliments to the
queen:

The laws of Charles the Fifth and Charlemagne,
Blessedly with their blood to her come down,
Shall make the whole world vassal to her crown

—a nice way of proclaiming the War of Devolution,
with sundry other wars. Mademoiselle Molière, in
turn, costumed as the Golden Century, proclaimed in
engaging disagreement that the goodness of "the wife
of Louis" was abolishing the horrors of war. As for
the "tireless hands" of which she reminded us, which
"were laboring without remission for the well-being
of humankind," no doubt they labored for the well-
being of the Versailles workingmen who were presently to perish in the miasmal swamps in order to rear
the palace at which we marvel.

The spectacle was rounded out with mechanical
contraptions, supernumeraries, and dummies. Particularly conspicuous were some reapers "clad appropri-
ately to their occupation, but very richly," and some
"aged men made of ice," whose frozen frailty it had
cost a pretty penny to reproduce. Then there appeared "a miniature mountain or cliff floating along in
mid-air in such wise that the device actuating it eluded
eyesight."

On May 8 *La Princesse d'Élide* was presented. This
was "a comedy with interpolated dancing and music"
that Molière had begun in verse but been obliged to
finish in prose; it was derived from a famous play by
the Spanish dramatist Moreto, about a princess who
had made a vow never to fall in love, but then surrendered to the young prince who pretended that he
had made the same vow. It is a mediocre comedy, all
on a dead level though of a dainty turn; after promis-
ing to be Shakespeare or to be Marivaux, it breaks its
promises without causing us any unbearable sorrow.
Because in it Molière played a clown who is something of a procurer, it has been surmised that he used
the play to remind the king of the obliging services
that Molière himself was now or formerly had been
able to render him. And indeed it is not inconceivable

that the king had had recourse to him, or that Molière had turned to account his favors to the sovereign.

Much more beguiling to the king than the comedy were the ring races and the head races. In these last a knight put his steed into full gallop and tried to impale with his lance a series of large heads distributed along the course. The king shone at this game, which was calculated to accentuate all the attractions of a man eager to seem appealing. Challenge after challenge kept it going for many rounds. Finally, grand climax of the celebration, came the destruction of Alcine's palace, which provided the occasion for a stupendous display of fireworks. A lottery did not yield the palm for lavishness to anything else; the prizes were precious stones, silver plate, and costly furniture. The coffers of France had sprung a leak, and out of it streamed the wealth of capitalists and merchants.

On May 12, in the midst of all this gold and splendor, by the blaze of torches and the blaze of jewels, in this ambient of artifice and eroticism, a black-clad man appeared on the stage and in a muffled voice delivered the lines that were to dumfound the age. The hearers were in a mood for every indulgence. The king was wholly intent on his Mademoiselle de La Vallière and the diamonds in his breastplate and the fiery plumes of his helmet and his pasteboard heads, though he had a judicious eye and a brain that always came awake when he needed it. A spectacle is a great deal more impressive than a reading; it speaks directly to the senses, and it signified nothing that the collar was shared between the priesthood and the judiciary, for it was not in the least the Parliament of Paris that Tartuffe's words conjured up. In the report printed by the *Journées* we read: "In the evening His Majesty caused to be enacted a comedy entitled *Tartuffe*, which Monsieur de Molière had written to expose hypocrites; but although it was found exceedingly entertaining, the king perceived so much likeness between those whom true devoutness had led

into the heavenly path and those whom a vainglorious
display of good works does not deter from practicing
evil ones, that his very great sensitiveness in religious
matters could not brook this resemblance between evil
and goodness, each of which might be mistaken for
the other; and although there was not the smallest
question of the author's good intentions, the king for-
bade public performances of the play and deprived
himself of a pleasure in order not to let others be led
astray who are less capable of forming an accurate
judgment of it." The phrasing seems prompted by
Molière if not supplied by him. Quite different was
the tone taken in the *Gazette* some days later. There
it was stated that the king had adjudged the play "a
sheer insult to religion and likely to lead to very dangerous results." The Society of the Holy Sacrament
was getting into action.

Louis XIV must have been listening to the Archbishop of Paris, Hardouin de Péréfixe, his former
teacher, even more than to his mother. This prelate
was not a member of the Society, but we know what
its underground machinations were. Molière lost no
time in lining up his defense. A fortnight of working
might and main to entertain the king deserved to be
rewarded, and what Molière needed was something
other than the 2000 livres he had received. He could
count, to begin with, on the co-operation of Madame,
whose influence was potent, and of Condé, who was
very far from sharing the opinions of his younger
brother Conti. A few days after the banning of *Tartuffe*, just after a scabrous play called *Scaramouche
Ermite* had been performed at court, the king had
remarked to Condé: "I should really like to know
why the ones that are so scandalized by Molière's
comedy haven't a word to say about this *Scaramouche*
comedy." And Condé had replied: "The reason is that
the *Scaramouche* comedy brings in heaven and religion, which are nothing to these gentry, whereas
Molière's comedy brings in these gentry themselves,
and that is what they won't put up with." A verdict

of that sort was an invaluable trump card to Molière. But despite the co-operation of Madame and Condé, neither of whom ever failed him during the entire campaign, despite the diplomatically favorable opinion of Cardinal Chigi, the legate *a latere*, to whom Molière read his play, and despite Molière's audiences with Louis XIV, in which sovereign and subject must have unbosomed themselves to each other with a degree of candor, the ban was not lifted.

Meanwhile the Society committed or tolerated a foolish blunder. Roullé, parish priest of Saint Barthélemy, published a frantic denunciation of *Tartuffe* in which he clamored for the consignment to the flames of both work and author. Imagine Molière's feelings. Roullé was no more a hypocrite than Bossuet was when, later on, he wrote the *Maximes sur la Comédie*. Molière, assailed in his repute, his self-respect, and his very moral being, was the target this time not of a scoundrel but of a bigot. And when, presently, Bossuet held forth, it was sincere devoutness that anathematized Molière. Was the figment of the sham devotee still tenable? Molière could not relinquish it. In his first petition to the king, of about August 15, he made an uncompromising declaration of the prerogatives of comedy. The task that he had taken upon himself was to denounce the vices of the age "by means of ludicrous portraitures." Vice was not inherently ridiculous: to make it so required the coloration that the painter supplied. This petition testifies to Molière's strong reliance, if not on the king's approval, at least on his own privilege of speaking freely to him. Implicit in the document are memories and reminders of private conversations. Roullé must have got himself pretty sharply reprimanded, for not long afterward we find him making clumsy apology. On September 14 the Society of the Holy Sacrament "passed a resolution to have anyone whom it might concern admonished to write nothing against the comedy *Tartuffe;* and they said that it was more to the purpose to ignore it than to denounce it, lest the author be driven to defend himself." Obviously not all the slings and arrows were aimed at Molière. The ban on the play continued, doubtless for substantial political and religious reasons, but the Society was by no means having everything its own way. It is very significant that the devotees were afraid of Molière's rejoinder—a proof that he was thought likely to be permitted to make it.

The princes were supporting Molière. On September 25 he acted *Tartuffe* for Monsieur at his Villers-Cotterets residence. On November 29 the five-act play, "finished and complete," was performed at Le Raincy at the residence of La Palatine, under Condé's sponsorship. The king is thought to have left Villers-Cotterets either the day before the performance there or on the very day of it.

The retort that the devotees were dreading was not long delayed. On February 15, 1665 the Palais Royal presented *Don Juan, ou le Festin de Pierre*, a play more daring than *Tartuffe* itself in its conception and its purposeful equivocations, and a frontal attack on hypocrisy. It had been played fifteen times by March 20. Apparently it was ordered discontinued before Easter. It was not published until after Molière's death. For the second time his vigorous initiative had been crushed. The blow was a severe one. The number of theatergoers was so limited that constant replenishment of theater fare was a necessity. Every play represented frozen capital. Molière worked with amazing speed, but he could not extemporize masterpieces. The company had to fall back on stale rubbish to replace the forbidden comedies, and the receipts fell off. However great the company's affection for Molière, it could not but sigh for the days when his works had not been a scandal that concerned the government and when the money had come rolling in. Into what outlandish regions was he venturing, this fine workman who had been so sure of himself and of other people when poking fun at harmless middle-class foibles? What were that churchman and that august noble doing on the comic stage, anyway? They were not at home there; they were a jarring element; they were upsetting. If only they had been heroes of tragedy, you could have shuddered over them in perfect comfort; but you had to laugh, and your laughter was poisoned by uneasiness. Molière as pilot of a fragile vessel that had no business to be on the high seas, Molière as a man well aware of his responsibility, was being worn down as much by others' worries as by his own.

He had, nevertheless, his compensations—not great enough ones to set everything quickly right, but still far from negligible. Louis XIV showed his sentiments about Molière and his attitude toward the controversy in a way as fair and as felicitous as possible. He asked his brother to make over to him the Palais Royal actors, and in the summer of 1665 Molière, summoned to Saint Germain, became leader of the king's company and was awarded an allowance of 6000 livres. Furthermore he had not stopped giving private readings of *Tartuffe*, and he acted the play a second time at Le Raincy. All manner of curiosity was aroused. By keeping it titillated—keeping the curtain half raised and disseminating reports that would multiply as time went on—the commercial value of the comedy was greatly enhanced. There was a hope that the ban was not permanent. Queen Christine of Sweden had heard *Tartuffe* talked about as far away as Rome, where she was making a retreat, and she wanted to have it performed in her private theater. Hughes de Lionne informed her that Molière was unwilling to risk making his play public property, lest he thereby lose the 20,000 écus that it might bring in "if he ever obtained permission to perform it"—a statement of the obvious.

Louis XIV's deference to his mother's views may have been one of the crucial factors in the banning of *Tartuffe*. Anne of Austria died in early 1666. But Molière had been ill from the end of the preceding autumn. The disease that was later to end his life had compelled him to leave the stage. The Palais Royal put on no performances from December 27 to February 21. Molière, coughing blood, was sentenced to a milk diet. Henceforth he would have to spare himself every possible exertion in order to weather the constant strain.

Everything was going badly. The king's favors imposed fresh obligations that Molière, now seriously ill, could not cope with. Every inch of ground that he relinquished was forthwith taken possession of by the opposition. As he saw it, his only salvation, his only hope of getting anywhere, was to be continuously on the spot, and illness meant above all else a calamitous absence. And his private life was not supplying him with any great consolations. To a man harassed as Molière was, domestic security is the nearest approach there is to happiness; but we shall see that Molière, whatever his wife's wrongs may have been, was a victim of jealous suspicions. We do not suffer less keenly or with less conviction of disaster from the troubles for which we are ourselves answerable than from those inflicted on us by others. There was nothing that Molière could rely on, no point at which he could relax.

On top of everything else, he had just quarreled with Racine in particularly unpleasant circumstances. Two years before, the young poet had brought Molière his *Thébaïde*, which the Hôtel de Bourgogne had shown signs of meaning to keep pigeonholed indefinitely. Molière had seen a chance to form a connection with a tragic poet who was to his liking—one whose works would constitute a complement to his own comedies and thus admirably round out the Palais Royal repertoire. Corneille and Molière represented too flat an opposition and, at the best, neutralized each other, but Molière and Racine showed two different facets of the same reality and made sense together. The two men had been meeting often and

intimately, and in the Left Bank taverns they, with
Boileau and La Fontaine, had been making a laughingstock of Chapelain in the name of the new aesthetics.
But Racine, being unconcerned about whatever had
no bearing on his own art and career, thought of the
Palais Royal as only a last resort. He greatly preferred
the Grands Comédiens' acting to that of Molière's
associates. On the evening of the fourth performance
of *Alexandre* at the Palais Royal, December 4, 1665,
the Hôtel de Bourgogne staged for the king, by a
secret arrangement with Racine, an alternative *Alexandre*. This maneuver enraged Molière's company,
which withheld Racine's percentage of the gate. Molière and Racine were equally ambitious and careerist,
but in different ways. Molière had the greater endow-
ment of moral energy, and it was generously ex-
pended; Racine was more niggardly of himself. Molière's fits of anger were fiery and outspoken, and
they took a social and moralistic turn, whereas Racine's
were icy. Both could be relentless, but whereas Molière's implacableness did not spare himself, Racine
apparently lacked the strength or the stamina for self-
criticism, at least in public. Racine's maneuver was
something more than a breach of comradeship. It was
painful to Molière, not as a piece of gratuitous malice,
but as a practical setback that happened to be painful.
It bore the stamp of a specialized vindictiveness that
took the form of stripping every vestige of fellow
feeling from a distressing truth, leaving the victims
disarmed, exposed, and helpless.

The year 1666 was to Molière a distressing one
throughout. The fine relaxed pace of his advance
slowed down, wavered, and stopped. The parts of the
machine that he had so skillfully assembled were jam-
ming and threatening to break. We see him thrown
back on himself, forced to supply the sustenance for
his work out of his own substance, letting himself
coast; losing his morale and then almost instantly re-
gaining it—amending it by a very wonderful comic
restoration. This year of his black depression and

deep discouragement, 1666, is also the year in which he set people laughing at *Le Misanthrope.*

He was not seriously to resume the offensive until the following year. The conditions were favorable. The king, more than ever surrendered to the pursuit of pleasure, was more than a little exasperated by the bigots. Monsieur de Montespan, daringly, was soon to decorate his private coach with a pair of horns. The more the king sinned, the more irritability he displayed. The Jansenist Barbier d'Aucourt had reviled *Don Juan:* to dispose the king favorably toward the comedy, now that his mother was no longer present to be outraged, no more was necessary than to give Orgon's remarks a Jansenist tinge, as Molière did not fail to do. The ever-faithful Madame was demanding a performance of *Tartuffe.* The Saint Germain festival was made the occasion for obtaining the king's permission; the least that can be said of his granting it is that it was obliging. Louis XIV having taken his burden of glory off to the army in Flanders, *Tartuffe,* or rather *Panulphe,* was presented to the public on August 5. The receipts were 1890 livres.

The hypocrite in the play had changed his garb along with his name. He was now a man of his time, and Molière had suppressed some actionable speeches and softened others. But it was all in vain. On August 6 a bailiff of the Parliament of Paris turned up at the Palais Royal at the instance of the *premier président,* Monsieur de Lamoignon. The play was prohibited all over again, and in terms that left scarcely any hope.

In the king's absence certain of his prerogatives devolved on the *premier président,* an upright man, but, as ill luck would have it, a member of the Society of the Holy Sacrament. He was an official in the grand style of the Parliament of Paris, at once tactful and unbending. Madame sent for him, but she got nothing out of him, and when he carefully abstained from mentioning the affair she did not venture to bring it up. Molière prevailed on Boileau to call on

Monsieur de Lamoignon with him. The author of *Le Lutrin* recorded for us a very suggestive account of the occasion:

"One morning we made our visit to Monsieur de Lamoignon, and Molière explained the object of his call. The *président* answered him as follows: 'My dear sir, I have a very high opinion of your deserts. I know that you are not only a superior actor, but also a very able man, a credit to your profession and to France. But with all my good will toward you I am unable to permit you to perform your comedy. I am convinced that it is very fine, very instructive; but it is not fitting for actors to be giving people instruction in matters of Christian morality and religion. It is not for the theater to get itself involved with the preaching of the gospel. When the king is back, he will permit you to act *Tartuffe* if it seems good in his eyes; but for my part I should see myself as abusing the authority that the king did me the honor to entrust to me during his absence, if I were to grant you the permission that you ask of me.' Molière, who was not expecting this declaration, was taken completely aback, in such wise that it was impossible for him to answer the *premier président*. He tried nevertheless to show the magistrate that his comedy was most harmless and that he had handled it with all the circumspection required by the delicacy of its theme. But Molière, try as he would, could only stammer, and he could by no means overcome the confusion into which the *premier président* had thrown him. That discreet magistrate, after listening to him a few moments, conveyed to him by a courteous refusal that he would not countermand the orders he had issued, and then he took his leave by saying: 'As you see, monsieur, it is almost noon; I should be missing mass if I were to linger any longer.' Molière withdrew, rather discontent with himself, but with no complaints to make about Monsieur de Lamoignon, for he had dealt justly. But all Molière's bad temper was directed at the Archbishop [de Péréfixe], whom he regarded as the ringleader of the faction of bigots that was opposing him." Molière confused, Molière stammering—that is as if a rope dancer were to stiffen and freeze; there could be no more distressful way of falling short. And he was wrong about the comparative importance of his opponents. It seems to me that this hearing throws a clear enough light on his discomfiture.

But nothing could stop him short of the last ditch. On August 8 La Grange and La Thorillère, the two trusty members of the troupe, took stage to make their way to the king in Flanders. They were the bearers of a second petition from their chief; in this one he threatened to forswear writing altogether if the faction proved to be more powerful than the royal benevolence. The emissaries were kindly received. Monsieur was accommodating, as ever, and the king made some promises not quite specific enough to eliminate every loophole. The journey cost a thousand livres. Simultaneously there was being distributed in Paris a *Lettre sur la Comédie de l'Imposteur*, very favorable to Molière, in which the philosophy of ridicule was expounded with noteworthy clearness. But almost at the precise time when Louis XIV was renewing his promises of support the Archbishop excommunicated everyone who should see or hear the play, *even at a guest performance*. As a matter of fact, this thunderbolt did not wreak much destruction. The excommunication itself was somewhat irregular; it was bound to nettle the king; and it is said that Péréfixe's ordination was revoked at the end of the year. But the demonstration of hostility was shattering. The Palais Royal shut its doors. Was Molière beginning to carry out his threat, or was he again laid low by illness? On December 25, "despite the squall and the tempest," as Robinet puts it, the Palais Royal repeated *Le Misanthrope*.

Molière had still to wait nearly a year and a half before he got the longed-for permission. But he did get it. At the beginning of 1669 the "Peace of the Church" appeared to have put an end to the Jansenist rebellion. The event was celebrated with state. Finally,

on February 5, *Tartuffe* under its proper title was
revived at the Palais Royal before an overwhelming
crush of people. There were twenty-eight consecutive
performances, and the comedy was acted twenty
more times before the year was out, in addition to
guest performances. In the ensuing years it was to be
played thirty more times before Molière's death. The
first edition, which cost one écu, was sold out in a few
days.

The organized fanaticism of the 1660's obscures for
us the real purport of *Tartuffe* and the real attitude of
Molière. Our own posterity, if it would know what
radical extremes French patriotism was capable of
in 1929, must not overlook the reading of *L'Action
Française;* but posterity will be making a mistake if it
looks to that organ for definitive information about
the patriotism of French statesmen. By the same token
it behooves us to weigh the pamphlets, lampoons, and
excommunications of the 1660's, and even the *Maximes sur la Comédie.* The war over *Tartuffe* brings
once more into the spotlight the inveterate irrecon-
cilability of earth and heaven. Not that Molière was
any less Christian than Boileau, or than the king. He
contrived to convince Louis XIV, and to convince
himself, that his religious sentiments were honest.
Even if we detect in him a detachment from religious
considerations that caused him to confuse fanatic with
scoundrel as objects of the same intolerance, and even
if a confusion of that sort was intolerable to the
Church from one who did not belong to it, it is still
no less true that fanaticism is a monstrous distortion
of Christian feeling. Monsieur de Lamoignon's reply
to Molière puts a finger on the real point of the contention. It sincerely represents the diplomatic argument as a valid argument: Molière is to be credited
with the best possible intentions, but he is politely admonished that it is not for the comic theater to get
itself involved with the preaching of the gospel. The
dispute over *Tartuffe* is a dispute over jurisdiction.

But behind the dispute over jurisdiction there is ambushed a much deeper issue, no more than glimpsed by Molière's contemporaries. It can be stated thus: Granted the entire good faith of the author, does not comedy, when it seizes upon the aberrations of religious emotion, entail a dislocation of the point of view that traduces religious emotion itself? In this area Molière's art bears the responsibility for his thinking. In composing his plays he worked from only a small number of scenic outlines. The probability is that similar moral relationships were associated in his mind with similar dramatic scenes. Now, there is one of Molière's comedies that shows some very striking parallels with *Tartuffe*. It is the comedy whose protagonist bears Orgon's very name, lacking one vowel. I am referring to *Le Malade Imaginaire*. Orgon and Argan are one and the same person subject to two different obsessions. The first is absorbed in his soul's salvation, the second in his body's well-being. This almost hypnotic obsession is due, in the one instance as in the other, to the sway of particular professional practitioners who have come to dominate the words and the actions of their patient, or victim. Each of the two wants to marry his daughter to the man who humors his aberration, and the comic genius, in the one instance as in the other, wears a servant's apron. Toinette exactly corresponds to Dorine; so exactly, indeed, that we find in *Le Malade Imaginaire* a scene repeated verbatim from *Tartuffe*—that in which Toinette says to Argan: "Gently! You do not bear in mind that you are ill," and Dorine says to Orgon: "Ah, you are devout, and you fly into tantrums!" Not until we get to the scenes between Orgon and Cléante in one play, and between Argan and Béralde in the other, does the correspondence break down, with the disparity that Béralde has not the same reasons for restraint that Cléante has. True, Monsieur Purgon is a man of genuine conviction, whereas Tartuffe is a hypocrite. But imagine a comedy that dramatizes a religious Monsieur Purgon: would it differ appreciably from the actual *Tartuffe* as far as its *comic purport* is concerned?

For the heart of the problem is precisely that point. Comedy recognizes no privileged vices. Very well: but is the failing chastised in *Tartuffe* hypocrisy? Rather, is it not excess of religious enthusiasm—as it were, the Christian hypertrophy of which Orgon is the victim? If Tartuffe is a hypocrite, comedy is not going to accomplish his reformation: at the best it will merely warn him that he will have to operate more discreetly—in other words, to make himself more of a danger to the weak. And if Tartuffe is *not* a hypocrite, then Molière stands deprived of his sole justification. With Orgon it is otherwise. He is honest, and he is befooled. The effects of Tartuffe's hypocrisy on Orgon's behavior are not, then, in the domain of hypocrisy. It is not in the least *because* Tartuffe is hypocritical that his victim is comic. Between Tartuffe's hypocrisy and Orgon's ridiculousness there is the bond of certain ideas, certain feelings—in short, a certain impulse that Tartuffe arouses. It is the impulse toward spiritual health, as with Argan it was to be the impulse toward temporal and corporeal health. It is the Christian impulse.

Any comic character, by Molière's theory, is an obsessed, a hypnotized person. His isolation, his helplessness to communicate with rational folk, his mental deafness and blindness, and his radiant happiness spring from an unwavering enthusiasm that keeps him under its spell. Sometimes in Molière this enthusiasm is self-sustaining, as with Arnolphe; sometimes it submits to the direct leverage of a social class, as with the Précieuses. But oftenest of all it brings into play a conscious or unconscious hypnotist who is manipulating puppets. The Sganarelle of *L'École des Maris* is the most self-sufficient of Molière's comic characters; he is hypnotized by his own conceit. Agnès hypnotizes Arnolphe by inadvertence and against her wish. Mascarille makes deliberate use of a hint already implicit.

Are the Précieuses less precious or less ridiculous because Mascarille is a fraud? Is Orgon less ridiculous—or less Christian—because Tartuffe is a fraud?

> Who heeds his words knows perfect peace within
> And counts as ordure all this world of sin.
> Yes, for his words a different man am I;
> He teaches me to shun each loving tie,
> From all mundane affections frees my life;
> I'd lose my brother, children, mother, wife
> Ere you should see me care as much as—that!

Scan this utterance of Orgon by itself for a moment. Forget the postures assumed; above all, forget Tartuffe. Then restore them to the comic framework and ask yourself what it was that you laughed at. It was simply the state of mind of a man utterly committed to the Christian way, severed root and branch from the world—the very state of mind that, when Pascal expresses it, gives you a spinal shiver. Now ask yourself why Orgon's words strike you as comic. You will recognize that Orgon is completely isolated with his soul at peace, that he has severed every connection with the natural, rational world—a characteristic, as we know, of the comic character, but also a characteristic (as we ought to know) of the Christian character. "Who can help laughing," Henri Estienne asks, "on reading that Saint Macaire did seven years' penance in thorns and thickets for having killed a flea?" It is laughter that casts the deciding vote. The Christian isolation becomes the paradigm of the comic isolation. What the ordinary human fervors become if a man loses his self-command and his sense of proportion, the Christian fervor becomes under the same provisos. But self-command and a sense of proportion are mundane values—mundane curbs that, as imposed in this comedy, are from a religious point of view entirely arbitrary.

The dispute over *Tartuffe*, then, is not *merely* a dispute over jurisdiction. Molière did not *merely* wish, as he declared, to castigate hypocrisy on the same terms as the other vices. Once started on this path, he could not avoid judging the Christian attitude itself in assigning it its place in human affairs. And we find him doing it in such wise as to lend color to a charge of epicureanism that he may actually not deserve. The value of any humanism rests on the terrestrial bases that it selects as defenses against the excesses of the godhead; but the very fact of having such bases throws it into an irreconcilable conflict with religion. For religion suffers us to live on this earth, but by no means to base our lives on it. Bossuet hits upon the crucial point when he cites Saint Augustine's distinction between the utility of the emotions on the one hand and addiction to the pleasures of sense on the other. But if a feeling—for example a healthy and vital love, or paternal tenderness, or a preference for self-restraint—seems to us good enough to curb the Christian fervor, how shall we forgo holding fast to it? This is the logic of Molière's fidelity to instinct, which is so effective because in it we descry his outraged astonishment and likewise his nostalgia. In *Tartuffe* he was thinking, not of Rabelaisian indulgences, but of those fastidious and tranquil emotions that attune with one another a group of privileged persons of sensibility. If he felt these emotions, he could hardly profess to be cultivating them. And anyone's denial or scorn of what seemed to him the best fortune open to mankind must have been intolerable to him.

The logic of comedy compelled Molière, possibly against his liking, to assail the very principle of the Christian religion, to make man stand erect by virtue of his own strength, and to throw himself on the mercy of his own instincts. The same logic carried him farther. Laughter has the inherent function of discharging the emotions, producing an emotional vacuum; it effects a kind of short circuit and changes the emotional sign from plus to minus. Consequently, it is a wonderful transcription of pain. All the themes of comedy are inherently painful or distressing or vexatious—anyway, hard to endure; they involve moderate everyday pain that plagues us not immoderately but chronically—such pain as laughter makes it possible to endure. And that is the point: that laughter is deliverance. Give the mechanism of laughter philosophical organization, and you oppose to religion an alternative method of enduring the world or of winning surcease from it. Saint Ambrose marveled that a Christian could bring himself to search for things to laugh at. Well he might. It is the search that raises the whole question; for it is a search, in the midst of the world and with worldly means, for forgetfulness and for deliverance. Once you stop passively succumbing to laughter as to a sneeze, once you make serious use of it to render this earth supportable, you set up a competition with religion that all Cléante's rhetorical disclaimers will never manage to disguise.

The logic of comedy, freed from the confining circle of its traditional subject matter, expanded to cover all the excesses of passion, had become, thanks to Molière's insight, a formidable tool—possibly even more formidable because he had not wished it to be.

Tartuffe once appraised, a choice has still to be made between two contrasting interpretations. We can imagine a freethinking Molière (he was reading *Tartuffe* at Ninon de Lenclos's house), but a diplomatic one (he had to retain the king's support), disguising his real feelings under a pretense of castigating noxious vices in a refined society; and we can also imagine Molière as an upright Christian fired with a kind of patriotic loyalty to the instincts as contrasted with the excesses of religious ardor, and discovering thereby the barrenness of his own Christianity. For my part I incline to the second theory. Molière's self-interest and his ideas are too inextricably involved for him to yield to a deliberate design to encourage freethinking. Moreover *Don Juan*, whatever may have been said of it, is nothing if not a critical portrait of freethinking, just as *Tartuffe* is a portrait of hypocrisy.

I do not believe that Molière, impatient and testy as he was, can have perceived—at first sight, anyway—the implications of his horror of a certain kind of devoutness. And he too may have been, in his own fashion, the dupe of a hypocrisy that presented to him in an opprobrious light a number of sentiments that he thought he did not directly attack in their central substance—a half conscious dupe who compliantly let himself be duped. No great philosopher, he may have thought that the golden mean, which he opposed to every kind of excess, defined a tenable position; the more so because some anything but moderate impulses of his own make-up made him see moderation as an ideal to be aspired to—rather the object of approval than a boon actually possessed. An ambitious artist with official standing, he had a self-interest in taking Cléante's pronouncements at face value and in representing a reasonable piety as no mask but a reality—a reality that validated the lofty pretensions of comedy.

But, quite apart from this ambiguity that Molière may or may not have perceived clearly, *Tartuffe* and *Don Juan* bear witness to a subtler and graver crisis—the primarily occupational crisis that I had in mind in remarking that thereby comic discernment comes into conflict with comic convention. *Don Juan* is the portrait of a great nobleman, *Tartuffe* that of a churchman, or a man who avails himself of ecclesiastical privileges. Don Juan is protected by the usages governing the nobility, Tartuffe by ecclesiastical interests. I am aware that Don Juan has been represented as Molière's mouthpiece, but a reckless and desperate skepticism must have seemed to him not much more endurable than saintly extravagances. What has this man in bondage to love of order, to jealousy, to the shifting image of a single woman, to a hundred middle-class prejudices, this man whose adaptability has the effect of extenuating his obstinacy—what has he in common with that rootless nobleman, that spendthrift whose idleness and arrogance have torn him out of the framework of ordinary humanity? No: what

Molière indicts before all else in *Tartuffe* and *Don Juan*, in connection with hypocrisy and with atheism, is *impunity*—a kind, or rather two kinds, of impunity that offended Louis XIV for reasons already touched on. And impunity, carried to its ultimate extensions, constitutes a problem that comedy is unequipped to solve.

Molière's favorite theme—one that, on the other hand, is within the province of comedy—is impunity punished; that is, the man who fancies himself untouchable and omnipotent, but upon whom the forces that he has himself unleashed recoil to crush him. If the lesson of comedy is to have free play—and it can operate only through the machinery of humor—the impunity must be a delusion of the ridiculous character, who is unwittingly contriving his punishment himself. The ridiculous character, blinded by a spell, persistently deceives himself at just the point where the audience, forewarned by the author, is not deceived; the delusion and the actuality, superposed, effect the dual vision that evokes laughter. On this system the audience is consistently in command of the character, and the more mirthfully in command in proportion as the character's fancied impunity arouses, through contrast and the vindictive instinct, that feeling of slight superiority that we require of comedy. In *Tartuffe* and *Don Juan* it is not the ridiculous character that boasts the impunity, and in them the comic lesson can therefore not be inexorably derived from the comic principle. If Orgon wielded the whole power of a paterfamilias, his authority could be diminished by contrivance, as Arnolphe's is. On the other hand, Tartuffe's arrogance—the arrogance that renders him comic, but comic in the fashion of a wordless gesture, without any disturbing laughter—and likewise the arrogance of Don Juan are of a sort altogether different from the arrogance of Sganarelle or of Arnolphe. So far from being under a spell, these are themselves the weavers of a spell; it is they that supply the comic motive power and exercise the dual vision that only author and spectator should possess. They are outside the framework of comedy by the same token that the author is—perhaps even more outside it than the author is, for he, deprived of his punitive apparatus, can only follow them where they choose to go. Here is the cause of the vast difference between the denouements of *Tartuffe* and *Don Juan* and the denouement of *L'École des Femmes*. The last-named is contrived but not inevitable; the other two are integral with the very design of the plays, and they disclose the predicament into which comedy has been sidetracked.

It does not seem to me that we can get out of the predicament by deciding with Brunetière that *Tartuffe* belongs to drama, or with other critics that *Don Juan*, at least through the elevation and the power of its hero, belongs to tragedy; for we can readily conceive of comedy as continuing to evolve in that direction without relinquishing either its discernment or its comic portraiture. And such an evolution was undoubtedly what Molière aspired to. The difficulty does not arise from the subject matter, already many times dealt with in comedy; the hesitancy is not that of Molière's hand, which has here a firmer grasp than ever. The fact that Tartuffe and, especially, Don Juan elude the correctional devices available to comedy means only that the audience had not the clue to truth and error that would promptly put it in command of these characters. The audience saw clearly enough that Tartuffe was hoodwinking Orgon and that he was wicked, but it did not see him fooling himself through his wickedness. It saw clearly enough that *he* was false, but it did not see that his pronouncements were false. It recognized the disquieting element in all Don Juan's power and in his cynicism, but when it saw that he was mentally superior to all the virtuous folk opposing him it no longer knew whether they or he had custody of the truth. And when the retribution *ex machina* took the audience by surprise it responded with angry resentment or mere astonishment, and not with laughter.

The underpinning of comedy is the comic convention whereby there is an accord, an identification, of error with vice and of truth with rectitude. The accord takes place, not in the mind of a solitary reflective reader, but in the spontaneous average opinion of a massed audience. This average public reasonableness is part and parcel of the comic conception itself, for it constitutes one half of the dual vision that the author needs in order to generate laughter. The comic poet of the theater is not the lord and master of his ideal: his ideal is supplied for him by the society that he is instructing only that he may lean the harder upon it. Molière might have found that support for *Tartuffe*—he did in fact find some of it—but the sobriety and the tensity of its portraiture were not fully counterbalanced, as in *L'École des Femmes*, by facile and forthright laughter; and in *Don Juan* the irresoluteness of the comic element becomes patent. Molière's mood is doubtless largely accountable for this quality: embattled, outraged, agitated, less self-confident than he pretends, he darkens the characters' features, and humor turns into satire. But it is still true that the more seriously he takes himself in the comic components, the more clearly he perceives the importance of a social rationale, a standard of truth external to himself, even though he had contributed more than anyone else to its formation.

Comic rationality and the average opinion of the audience no longer coalesce into a single actuality. For this fusion Molière had wrought with all the strength he could muster. For the full realization of his art and his thinking he needed certainty, and if the judgment of laughter were to be spontaneous the certainty had to be unquestionable and obvious. But such public participation is never possible without some degree of compromise. Truth, yes; but it has to be adjusted to the credos of a given society. Certainty, yes; but it has to be restricted and rigidified by the simplifications of the multitude. Molière believed that by forming this indispensable alliance with the public he could simultaneously exploit his business, his career, and his genius. At the precise juncture at which his genius was threatened with loss of balance, worries of every description were turning it momentarily against its natural ally. *Le Misanthrope* is a revolt against comedic wisdom, against the society represented by the audience—a revolt that is promptly quelled, and within the work itself. For *Le Misanthrope* ends in a victory of the public, a victory of comedy after the early threat to it. Swept away by his mood, torn by worries and delays and setbacks to which he was unused, Molière felt that within the established boundaries of comedy he was suffocating. By means of the same bold foray that delivered Tartuffe and Don Juan from comic castigation, he meant to emancipate himself from comic approval and on it to vent his fury. But thanks to the leverage of the public, thanks to the necessity of expressing himself in the language of his own choice, of which he had gained a superb mastery, and by virtue of his innate sympathy with a purely human and mundane wisdom, he found that he had to subject his anarchic mood to exactly the same controls against which it was revolting. We shall see how, by dint of this rigorous discipline, applied this time to himself rather than to others, he came on the discovery of a still deeper comic rationality and of a ridicule that is for all time.

CHAPTER SIX

ALCESTE

I stop at nothing, you shall see; I mean
To prove it myth that humankind is wise—
And every heart will do what in it lies.

LE MISANTHROPE

THE STRUGGLE over *Tartuffe*, from the very outset, had been made the more painful to Molière by both private miseries and professional worries. The repertoire was a problem; there were vexations at the theater; du Parc died November 4, and on the 10th came the death of little Louis, firstborn of Molière's children. Late autumn brought forth galling sequels to an old lawsuit that dated from the period of the Illustre Théâtre—annoyances mild and not so mild that were aggravated by the stress of trying to regain a balance jeopardized in some critical ways; aggravated by foundered hopes, by harrowing reminders.

The year that followed yielded some few gratifications—the birth of a daughter, Esprit-Madeleine; the triumph of *L'Amour Médecin;* above all, the king's personal patronage. But Molière was struck down by illness, and apparently he was hounded at intervals by doubts—doubts about the genuineness of his powers, the legitimacy of his hopes; doubts about what was truth; doubts about the comic understanding; doubts about Armande; self-doubts. If we consider that doubt is the mental counterpart of marking time, and that the comic genius has not the privilege of self-distrust, we shall gain an inkling of Molière's inward turmoil. There are men of stature who do not feel fully alive unless they are in a state of indecision, but to Molière that state was a disaster and a torment. Between 1664 and 1666, when he was at the bottom of the abyss in both material circumstances and mood, he conceived and wrote *Le Misanthrope*. It is the work of a man who, for the time being at least, no longer knows where he stands in relation to goodness and truth, justice and reason—a man floundering in one of those spiritual fogs that all of us, in some chapter of our lives, have to work our way through.

During the Versailles festival of 1664 Molière's earliest marital mishaps were brought back to life by scandalmongering. Armande, dazzled by flattery and luxury, intoxicated by the splendor of her own surroundings and swayed by the eroticism that dominated even the king, was supposed shamelessly to have succumbed. Names mentioned were those of Richelieu, Guiche, and the amazing and enigmatic Lauzun. Dutiful biographers have had the satisfaction of proving that both Richelieu and Guiche were far away from Versailles at the time, and tradition has pronounced the remaining candidate, Lauzun, proof against Armande's ardors. But why set store by the tittle-tattle of that hotbed of gossip? Does it need the most irresistible lordlings of the court to account for the consummation of the spiritual divorce so graphically exposed in *L'École des Femmes?* Was the estrangement between Molière and his wife a consequence of the wife's betrayal? Is it not by ourselves, unassisted, that we wreak the cruelest betrayals on those who love us but whom we do not love?

Two contemporary reports of conversations show the relationship of Molière and Armande in different lights that can be seen as either contradictory or complementary—reports couched in seventeenth-century terms and careless of factual truth while deferential to spiritual truth. Between them they are responsible for all the interpretations that have been made of these shadowy recesses of Molière's life. I want to put the two conversations before the reader before I propose an interpretation of my own.

In a pamphlet violently hostile to Molière's wife an anonymous writer either reports or imagines a dialogue in which Molière confides in Chapelle, who chides him for weakly succumbing to his passion:

"Chapelle, who considered himself above that kind of mischance, heaped derision on the circumstance that anyone so proficient as Molière in depicting other men's infirmities should himself fall into the very infirmity that he was consistently satirizing, and he demonstrated to Molière that the crowning absurdity was loving someone who did not return one's fondness for her. 'For my part,' he told Molière, 'I assure you that if I were unlucky enough to get into such a fix and were solidly convinced that the woman in question granted her favors to other men, I should feel such contempt for her that it could not fail to cure me of my infatuation. You actually have an advantage that would not be yours if it were a matter of a mistress. When a man's affections are trampled on, his love is generally supplanted by vindictiveness, and that could relieve you of all the miseries that your wife inflicts on you, because all you have to do is lock her up—a conclusive way to set your mind at rest.'

"Molière, who had listened to his friend with passable composure, broke in here to ask Chapelle if he had never been in love.

" 'Yes, I have,' Chapelle rejoined—'as much as a sensible man has any business to be. But I would never have made any such to-do over something that my own dignity admonished me to do, and I blush for you that you should be so irresolute.'

" 'It is clear to me,' Molière told him, 'that you have never loved. You have mistaken the mere semblance of love for the reality. I will spare you a thousand illustrations that would bring home to you the imperiousness of the tender passion; I will only give you an unvarnished account of my own predicament, that you may get an idea how helpless we are when love asserts such mastery over us as our particular temperament permits.

" 'As to this complete knowledge of the human heart that you say I have, judging by the characterizations of it that I am constantly exhibiting, I will grant you that I have striven as earnestly as in me lay to plumb its weaknesses. But if my knowledge has taught me that it is in our power to fly from danger, my own experience has made me perceive only too clearly that there is no way to escape it. I always judge these matters with reference to myself. My inborn tendency is to be extremely affectionate, and, thinking that my fervor would be able to awaken feelings in her that would become second nature and would be lasting, I overlooked no efforts to that end. Since she was young when I married her, I did not recognize her evil bent, and I considered myself a little less unfortunate than the general run of those who take on such responsibilities. What is more, being married did not lessen my assiduity. But in her I met with such coldness that I began to see how futile had been all my vigilance. I saw that the most she felt for me had been far short of what I would have wished for my own happiness. I took myself to task for a forbearance that seemed to me ridiculous in a husband, and I put down to her perverse mood what was actually a result of her want of affection for me. But I found only too many opportunities to discover my mistake; and before long her wild infatuation for the Comte de Guiche made such a scandal that I could not keep up my show of equanimity.

" 'When I learned of the affair I did everything I knew how to get myself in hand, finding it hopeless to make her any different. I gave my whole mind to that endeavor; I invoked the help of everything that could give me solace. I viewed her as someone whose worth lay solely in her purity—someone whose faithlessness was making her repulsive. I made up my mind that I would live with her thenceforth in the way of any decent man with a light-minded wife, in the conviction that, whatever others may say, his dignity is entirely independent of his wife's misbehavior. But I had the mortification to find that a woman who was no beauty—and who owed such mental capacity as she exhibited to what I had taught her—was wrecking all my philosophizing at a touch. Her nearness made me forget my resolve, and a few words of hers in self-extenuation left me so persuaded of the baselessness of the charges that I asked her to forgive me for having been so gullible.

" 'My indulgence, however, made not the slightest difference to her. If you realized what I am going through, you would be giving me your pity. I am so carried away by my infatuation that I actually sympathize with her propensities, and when I contemplate how impossible it is for me to conquer my feeling for her I tell myself that by the same token it may be equally hard for her to suppress her own innate tendency to dalliance, and I catch myself rather pitying than reproaching her. You are going to assure me, I dare say, that this is a sort of love proper only to a father: well, for my part I hold that there is only one kind of love and that those who have never known a trace of such qualms have never truly loved. As far as I am concerned everything in creation involves her. My brain is so surcharged with her that when she is away from me I can't think of a thing that would beguile me. When I look at her, such ferments as a man can feel but not express deprive me of all power of reasoning; I no longer have any eyes for her faults, and all I can see in her is her lovable qualities. Is not this the last word in lunacy? Does it not seem strange to you that whatever sense of logic I possess avails only to make me realize my helplessness without being able to overcome it?' "

Grimarest, in turn, records the following declarations by Molière to his friends Rohault and Mignard:

" 'Do you not pity me,' he said to them one day, 'for being in a calling and in a personal situation so at loggerheads with my present feelings and state of mind? I am fond of an unruffled life: yet my own life is disrupted by endless commonplace disturbances on which I never reckoned in the beginning, and I have to be totally engrossed in them, willy-nilly. After all the foresight that a man can exercise I have not escaped tumbling into the quagmire into which anyone generally does tumble when he marries in haste.'

" 'Dear, dear!' said Monsieur Rohault.

" 'Yes, my dear Monsieur Rohault,' Molière went on, 'I am the unluckiest man alive, and I have got only what I deserved. It never occurred to me that I was too exacting for family life. I thought my wife ought to let her behavior be regulated by her own virtue and by my wishes—and I see perfectly that as things stand for her she would now be even unhappier than I am if she had done so. She is a gay person, a sprightly person, and she enjoys making the most of those qualities; but all that sort of thing makes me sulk in spite of myself. I blame her for it; I take her to task about it. Being a woman infinitely more reasonable than I am, she wants the pleasant enjoyments of life. She goes her own way, and, secure in her own innocence, she scorns to submit to the restraints that I urge on her. This airy indifference I construe as defiance. I crave some evidences of affection, so that I can believe she feels some; and I should like her to be more circumspect in her behavior, to set my mind at ease. But my wife, being equable and serene in her own mind—and she would be invulnerable to all suspicion on the part of any man less excitable than I am—leaves me to my self-torment without mercy. Intent only on her wish to please everybody, like all her sex, and with no designs on anybody in particular, she made a mock of my susceptibility. If only I were able to enjoy my friends' company as often as I could wish, to take my mind off my troubles and worries— But your unavoidable engagements and my own preclude that consolation.'

"Monsieur Rohault favored Molière with all the apothegms of a wholesome philosophy by way of demonstrating that it was wrong for him to give in to his distresses.

" 'Oh,' Molière rejoined, 'I should never manage to play the philosopher to a wife as enchanting as mine is; and if you were in my shoes you might go through some pretty thorny passages yourself.' "

The romantic commentators, and pre-eminently Sainte-Beuve, have banked on the first of these conversations. Molière's disclosures to Rohault were too restrained and insufficiently histrionic to suit them. It may be that the two colloquies match two different stages in Molière's moral growth or two of the harried husband's different tempers. A man who feels competent to state his wife's case more truthfully than would be possible to an outsider may assume her defense as an obligation the more imperative in proportion as his temper goads him into unfairness to her in their private spats. Also, I am aware of the crucial weakness of these testimonies, which is that they were set down, not before *L'École des Femmes* and *Le Misanthrope*, but after them. It does not matter. We look to them, not for attestation of biographic facts, but for interpretations of Molière's inner self. And his disclosures to Rohault impress me as being, of the two, the more compatible with his feelings as revealed in his writings.

We see him as innately jealous and apprehensive; and the proof that so he was is to be found in his selection of Don Garcie as leading character when he decided to try his hand at the serious drama in a period when he was still managing to cling to his illusions about Armande. What we have here, it would seem, is the procedure of a man who, as prelude to depicting human nature in its deeper and more dramatic aspects, undertakes a searching self-analysis— not, assuredly, in an impulse to publicize his own woes, but to make use of what is troubling him in a play that shall work on the emotions. This jealous apprehensiveness, an apprehensiveness that conjured up ogres, would seem to have invested Molière's emotional life with its characteristic color and rhythm. The trouble he took over his wife's education is decidedly a jealous man's expedient. There ensued his realization of a congenital incompatibility, of an inherent maladjustment and its irony—of the impersonal ruthlessness of one person's ruling impulse to the ruling impulse of another. From the two conversations we extricate precisely that concept of the impotence of reason to which Molière's work as a whole bears witness. In both, an inborn incompatibility is cited as the ultimate cause of misunderstanding. It is noteworthy, too, that in the pamphlet in which Armande stands charged with all manner of derelictions Molière is made to expatiate on her infatuation for Guiche but says not a word about physical infidelity. The propensity to be jealous, the reasoned struggle to stand firm against it, the mockery of this struggle, the mockery of jealousy itself as a force that the jealous man can neither submit to nor suppress—these, it seems to me, are among the signposts that we can follow without the least likelihood of going astray.

Whether Armande was or was not physically unfaithful to her husband is a side issue. Her being unfaithful in act would not greatly have aggravated her spiritual infidelity. And, anyway, can we speak of unfaithfulness in one who had apparently never been faithful? We surmise that there was, underlying the mental conflict, a physical maladjustment—a very serious matter to a man organized as Molière was. Jealousy is not in every instance so egocentric as is assumed. Many a jealous man suffers less from sharing a woman's favors with others than from his own incapacity to provide her with every gratification. Frustrated longing to give unquestionably entails worse torments than frustrated longing to receive, so direct and insistent is its impotence. An aspect of Armande's flirtatiousness that may have nettled Molière more painfully than the enjoyment she took in the society of others was her capacity for getting along without him. And he may have suffered still more through the effect of marital tension on his inmost life. A man ceases to take pleasure in himself when in his whole being he has to make shift without the integration that he has achieved in his intellect.

Molière, constrained to recognize the inexorable tyranny of the senses and the impotence of reason, rebelled wholeheartedly against this recognition. Comic portraiture, we have seen, presupposes a very well defined, very concrete acceptation of truth, to the end that the representation of reality may enable us instantly to pronounce the character's behavior a sham. The comic sphere is the domain of sin; but it is likewise the domain of error. For that reason it is a domain patterned, as it were, by reason, which takes satisfaction in branding its illogicalities; and by virtue of the dual vision that provokes laughter we can put it that in comedy the truth is made use of in order to express error. To this extent comedy in its human roots is a makeshift, a defeat of reason; reason fails to have its way with the world, but retaliates on the world by describing it panoplied in all its absurdities. There is no comic insight where there is no clash between reason and actuality, or where reason is not powerless to amend life. Whence the confusion implicit in the celebrated claim of comedy to be a reformer of humankind. To be sure, it can reform people in the sense of instructing them to disguise their ridiculousness; but when it comes to destroying the attributes that make them ridiculous, thereby rising to the status of a social force, that is no more than an unattainable aspiration.

These observations will perhaps suggest how, in Molière, creative impulse and personal temper become one. He could produce those masterpieces at which we marvel because he possessed an enjoyment and a grasp of reason and also, at the same time, a deep conviction of its impotence to regulate human affairs; because his reasoning faculty and his temperament, equally unyielding, collided head on instead of joining forces; because he was exercising his sovereignty over a specialized audience that was unanimous in its definitions of the true and the false; because, finally, it was an age in which everybody believed the world to be unchangeable. Let us not be misled by appearances.

Louis XIV's reign is also the reign of disbelief. (I mean, of course, disbelief in the intellect.) The palace at Versailles, a comedy by Molière, and a tragedy by Racine are precisely equivalent expressions of the wholesale retreat from reason, a force that no more presides over mankind than the honorary chairman presides over an assemblage. Reason has ceased to be a working model and become a mold; and the mold eventually confers its own dignity on the exaltation of unreasoning impulse. In Molière, however, the abdication of reason is but partial. Retaliation is, after all, one kind of compensation. A whole congeries of attendant circumstances, inward and outward, must work together if the comic insight is to attain its consummate development; and for this reason Molière's private disasters have an appreciable bearing on the history of comedy itself. *Le Misanthrope* is at once an adventure of the comic intelligence and an adventure of Molière as an individual.

This composite adventure amounts to the projection of the author into the comic world that he has himself created—his recognition that he is part and parcel of it. Having detected in his own personality the discrepancies that he has satirized in others, he administers to himself the baptism of ridicule. We have seen how that nemesis of the comic spirit, skepticism, overshadowed *Tartuffe* and, even more completely, *Don Juan*. The drama of this skepticism and of its collapse under the castigation of comedy forms the theme of *Le Misanthrope*. Alceste's logic is in contention with the logic of comedy; and whatever occasional doubts we may experience when we read *Le Misanthrope*, Molière's contemporaries experienced none. Alceste the good man is no antithesis of Tartuffe the bad man, and neither is he a counterpart of Don Juan as one "beyond good and evil": he is, to the very marrow, a comic figure of the line of Arnolphe. From first to last he is subservient to the point of view of the seventeenth-century spectator. Whereas in *Tartuffe* and *Don Juan* wickedness and evil were stronger than social consciousness, in this play virtue is invariably weaker than the leverage of society. But what makes Alceste ridiculous, or at least justifies the ridicule of him, is not his defense of virtue by comic expedients, nor yet his infatuation with a light woman. Célimène and society merely furnish the apparatus for uncovering in him a more ingrained, a congenital ridiculousness. Here once more it is to Molière's work that we have to look for light on his manner of thinking and on the basic pattern of his life.

The name Alceste he derived from a Greek word denoting a man of strength, a powerful champion. Strength, power, is one of the inherent attributes of the character. Witness the action of the opening act, the onset in the second, the culminating scene of Act IV. Alceste is a man of onsets, a trampler—the sort of fighter who, in the prize ring, would be always boring in. The sonnet scene is conducted in the manner of a bout, with series of jolts shorter and shorter in range, more and more telling, hammered home by the rhythm of the lines.

Alceste is a man of abrupt and total outpourings, a man who explodes. He is of a solidity that by contrast renders everything outside himself insubstantial, transparent. He is as quick as he is strong, as witty as energetic. He hits upon the *mot juste* with stunning speed.

> Nor should I now be giving you a thought
> If elsewhere my revenge were better sought.

How answer so direct a thrust? Alceste arrogates to himself the privilege of starting a rumpus about anything and everything without regard to the consequences—the one privilege to which Molière could lay no claim. To that extent Alceste is the antithesis of Molière the professional man and courtier—the Molière who was driven to elaborate disguises of his opinions to get them tolerated and to dancing attendance on judges in an effort to win lawsuits; the Molière who (as Donneau de Visé tells us) "with a dexterity peculiar to himself consistently implied more than he said." But Alceste, precisely because he is the antithesis of Molière, is surrogate for a Molière freed from his trammels, a Molière whose station in life entitles him to outspokenness and who can treat himself to the indulgence of flatly defying the entire human species in lieu of paying it off by the circuitous method of having it stumble into comic snares. Molière beset, brought up short at every turn by the gesturing motley of such Bores as he celebrated in *Les Fâcheux*, constrained by discretion and by ambition to hold his peace—how can he, freed of the last restraint, vent once for all so immense an accumulation of dudgeon and impatience? How can he, once for all, nerve himself up to the highest pitch, as some men relax their tensions? Do it he can: he does it in the outbursts of Alceste.

This was but the first time that he had so let himself go. The workman with his trade to ply, his balance to preserve, the human being under his load of assorted responsibilities, gave himself up to this explosion of temper. But he did not enjoy it. It rasped him; it plagued and confused him. He was very familiar with the special discomfort of such harassments. It is always occasioned by one or another kind of excess. But it had commonly been the excesses of other folk that irked him. Now the immoderation was in a sense his own. Among the Bores was one that would not let him alone even when he had contrived to give all the rest the slip—one that followed him home, to confront him again in his privacy. In his instinctive struggle to rid himself of the invader he had at first no inkling of the source of his agitation. Righteous indignation, reasoning faculty outraged—it was all one. He no sooner caught himself in extravagance than, by the inveterate habit of his craft, he saw himself as warped. And he could not imagine himself thus disordered except as a figure in a comic pattern. He did not possess a Rousseau's knack of making the most of his resentment to evoke from it a world refashioned.

There could be no outlet but ridicule. Ill temper was to stand condemned by the very act of venting itself —condemned under the penal code that rules over comedy. The uproar raised by Alceste was to be swallowed up in the even more thunderous uproar of laughter.

Molière and Alceste—they are playing the same part. Broken is that collaboration of reason and passion that flowers in the comic creation. Alceste and Molière are self-divided. Alceste is a Molière who has lost his awareness of the comic; in other words, his power to maintain his discernment in defiance of his temper. He can no more laugh at himself than he can at others. He has an outlook on life that is precisely Molière's, but he cannot turn it into comedy. He exhibits, then, all the stigmata of the comic figure, but in an entirely novel way. Whereas the comic figure had been cut off from the world by his unreason, Alceste is cut off from it by his reasonableness and his goodness—qualities that he has in excess, to be sure, but for their excess society is at least as much to blame as his own make-up.

> I want straightforwardness and upright dealing
> And no word said except from honest feeling.

In those lines you have a virtuous temper on a reasoned basis, only the reasoning has no congruity with such comic reasoning as shapes the social order at which he lashes out. And here is a major new departure. Social comedy is invariably an analysis of individuality, and the comic figure is invariably an individual; but he is an absurd individual, not for a moment capable of maintaining his position. Here, on the contrary, is a ridiculous person triple-armored in reason, occupying positions defensible by logic; a completely integrated, self-contained individual who stands or falls by an interpretation of himself that flatly contradicts the comic interpretation.

> My word, good sirs, I never thought to find
> Myself so ludicrous.

It is in such challenges that we must read the riddle of the Misanthrope—the valiant fighter who begins by proclaiming to Philinte: "So much the worse for anyone that laughs!" However devoid of the comic perception, he is perfectly aware that he can become an object of ridicule; and he means to prove that a man can rise to withstanding the comic spirit and nullifying it, and that goodness is more powerful than society.

Alceste is wrong: society is more powerful than goodness. And it is so, not by virtue of a cowed playwright's fawning on his audience, but through an inevasible law. Society—or the comic intelligence—reflects a person's own likeness back to him. Alceste will have none of this distorting mirror; it makes him close both his eyes and his fists. But he thereby quite ceases to see himself and hence to examine himself. His reasonableness and his goodness had had no props outside himself, and he is therefore no longer able to distinguish their dictates from those of his own ego. His idiosyncrasies appear to him as revelations vouchsafed by reason, his fits of temper as righteous inspirations. His "I mean to be noticed," flung at Philinte, is just as material to him as his "I—I mean to get angry." His sapience is merged into his irascibility, is appropriated by it. At first he will have it that nobody is the least bit evil; now he will have it that nobody is the least bit reasonable. On that system this exasperated reformer ends by playing into the hands of his enemies. In future he will be contributing more than most men toward keeping the world exactly the way it is. Such is the first of society's triumphs.

For a second triumph more sweeping than the first, society bides its time. It is possible for an individual, intead of shutting his eyes, to muster enough strength to shatter the mirror that a given society is, in order to put another in its place. It will always be averred after the fact that a society can be transformed when its rules penalize or outrage men's best attributes. But there remains, deep within and inexpugnable, the inconsistency that the person once self-deceived detects in his behavior; and what manner of revolution is to extirpate that? The Misanthrope recognizes this contradiction in himself, and his "undying" hatred and his flight into the wilderness are partly dictated by disappointment in himself—major facts too often overlooked. In other words, Alceste becomes transformed; even in his own eyes he is not the man at the end that he was at the beginning; and when he gives up the struggle he is overthrown as much by his own verdict as by society's.

The story of Alceste is primarily the story of a will power that goes bankrupt. Note how, in the early acts, he expresses himself persistently and vehemently in the language of volition: "I want people to be straightforward," "I mean to get angry." He seems to have no doubt that a man can regulate his behavior according to his will, and this belief curiously increases the severity of his judgments of people. This vigorous man, this vehicle of an unacknowledged reasonableness, is contending for something more than mere reasonableness: he is trying to wrest Célimène away from a world of depravities, and he battles as he does because he possesses self-confidence, and he has self-confidence because he believes that he is loved. It would be difficult to overestimate the significance of this interchange between Alceste and Philinte:

> "You think she loves you, then?"
>   "Deuce take it, yes!
> Should I be loving her if I did not?"

Here is the will as Corneille conceived it, playing its part in the life of the emotions, projected into the future in the shape of a possibility that the character relies on and thinks of as making sense of his life. He bets on his will; over and above that he lives on advances against a capital fund of heroism that he takes for granted. The different parts notch into one another; on Alceste's behavior in relation to Célimène depends the justification of his attitude throughout the play. But there ensues Célimène's betrayal, followed by an appalling reversal on the part of Alceste. Here is the moment for him to be the man he thinks he is. First, then, in a gesture of magnificent rage he lays down the law to his emotions by offering his heart to Éliante. Enter Célimène. She displays sham feeling; she quibbles frivolously; she calculates the odds; she flings taunts; she is first evasive and then arrogant; in short, she does everything that would tend to harden Alceste's determination. But what do the dictates of the will amount to now? How perfectly the lines borrowed from *Don Garcie* fit this situation! and, because they are grounded in truth, how devastatingly! Here we have Arnolphe facing Agnès all over again, but now without the comic attendant circumstances: the ridiculousness this time only reinforces the inexorable interplay of the feelings.

Alceste's frustration culminates in the closing scene:

> With all my mind I swear to wish you ill—
> But how to make the heart obey the will?
> (*To Éliante and Philinte*)
> What lengths ignoble fondness drives us to!
> My weakness I make plain to both of you.
> But, truth to tell, the end you have not seen.
> I stop at nothing, you shall see; I mean
> To prove it myth that humankind is wise—
> And every heart will do what in it lies.

Here he is no longer the same person, not only because he is suffering torments through his love, but also because his love has just shown him his kinship with the monsters of that pit in which the vices hold sway—a discovery that he owes to his perception of what in him lies and to his loss of trust in his own will power. And in the final terms proposed by Alceste and rejected by Célimène do we not descry a half conscious expedient for recovering the conviction that his life makes sense? a sort of tacit license that he confers on himself to resume the language of volition and the appearance of complying with it?

This closing stage for Alceste is also the closing stage for a whole era—the swan song of the creative will, of transcendentalism in love. Rousseau, exclusively intent on mirror-shattering, misconceived the central purport of *Le Misanthrope:* to wit, that there is in every human being an incorrigible comic nucleus —various components of inconsistency and self-deception that no imaginable reconstitution of society could abolish. Moreover, the Comic Muse achieves a neat retaliation by letting us behold the misanthrope of Montmorency impelled by some extremely dubious moral considerations to charge Molière with having belied Alceste. Obviously Alceste, if he truly wants to enforce his own reasonableness, will have to take both himself and his world with equal seriousness. Let him become a Jacobin, and instead of fleeing the world and betaking himself to a wilderness he will convert the world itself into a wilderness. He will no longer comprehend that the power of reason is being used to make endurable precisely the things that he was formerly determined to reform by reasonable means.

Le Misanthrope was first played June 4, 1666. The comedy was apparently well received by literary and court circles, but its popularity was rather short-lived. It is tacitly ranked as a play for connoisseurs; but when we find so accomplished a connoisseur as André Gide disturbed by this masterpiece we wonder if *Le Misanthrope* has not some other shortcoming than excess of subtlety. The truth is that this comedy in which the comic principle itself is endangered embodies an inescapable ambiguity. Alceste's outcries give the case away. Molière, in the costume of the part, evoked laughter; but today's audience no longer laughs at *Le Misanthrope*. It is as essential to record this fact as it is to note of a picture that time has darkened it. The analogy breaks down at the circumstance that what has darkened *Le Misanthrope* is the change in our own understanding. The play was written with the co-operation of a social order that

Molière could assume to be static. Evolutionary social processes have changed everything.

A work of art may undergo modification in either of two different ways. The first is by succumbing *in toto* to the passage of time, as Voltaire's tragedies have done; the second is by giving off quite new resonances on contact with a new perceptiveness. In the second event—which applies to *Le Misanthrope*—the cause of the change seems almost without exception to be our inability to keep on receiving the subject matter in the aesthetic framework originally given it. We no longer concede that the way in which we see the subject matter expressed is an admissible way of expressing it.

For one example, we have become nowadays exceedingly captious about the constructions put upon exalted emotions. It is not that we have better morals than the seventeenth century, but we do have the hesitancies, the squeamishness, and the snobbery that go with our morals. And we do not at all grant that the highest values become devaluated in a society that seems to us at once despicable and improvable—a society in which we who compose it are more religious than Molière's generation. We no longer feel that we are incarcerated: we contrive all manner of gateways of escape. These exits, to be sure, might not serve us in an emergency, but we take comfort in knowing that they are there. It is an unhappy propensity. Because we think that everything is sure to be adjusted—or maladjusted—we presently lose our awareness of the element in each of us that is forever unadjustable, and we sink to a lower level thereby.

Nor is that all. We have observed how strained are Arnolphe's emotions in *L'École des Femmes*. The strain is compensated by the strictness of the sentence that comedy pronounces on them, but the strain is none the less felt. In *Le Misanthrope* this strain is even greater; at times it becomes downright cramp. Now, traditionary comedy inclines to expansiveness and relaxation. Laughter dilutes or destroys pain through the instrumentality of reason. It is, then, natural enough that laughter should be among the weapons of a philosophy that aspires to apply reason to the avoidance of pain. The philosophy that so aspires is epicureanism. All good and all evil, Epicurus avers, subsist through the senses; but our ways of thinking compel us to invoke reason for taking account of this basic fact. All pleasure is a good, but the consequences of pleasure may entail an evil that outweighs the good of the pleasure itself. At this point reason has to be invoked afresh for selection and appraisal of the various goods in life. The prime necessity being to forestall inward storms and stresses—to keep the body released from pain and the mind from turmoil— the supreme good would appear to be discretion. The wise man chooses virtue because it is the prerequisite of all enduring pleasure. And he is enabled to choose, to have preferences, only because he is free. The epicurean rationale constructs a world apart from the everyday world—one in which all uproar is subdued, absorbed into a sedate harmony; one into which sensory experience can come only when emptied of all its content that is troublous or anguished.

In Lucretius—with whom Molière was familiar— we perceive how the comic spirit and the epicurean doctrine merge. For this least comic of mortals adjures us to regard the disquiets of our kind as "food for laughter, for sheer derision." The rational will has vanished from the world of the philosopher, and what he finds left in it is only a succession of scenes whose tragic purport has its roots in a mildly ludicrous haphazardness. The later Greek comedy and its Latin progeny usher their audience at bargain rates into the Garden of Epicurus. On the comic stage all ties are loosened, all distinctions dissolved; nothing leads to anything, and everything fuses with everything else. In that domain we find ourselves a world away from such a comedy as *Le Misanthrope*, in which the incarnation of wisdom, Philinte, participates in the action, and the ridiculous protagonist is an embodiment of virtue, and his very virtue makes cracks appear here and there in the comedic varnish, and the working out of the comic theorem becomes rigorous and implacable. Schlegel had no esteem for this patterned austerity; he thought it subversive of the comic values. He ranked Molière's farces above the comedies, and in the farces he preferred the episodes of pure fantasticality.

But Schlegel's criticism holds good only if we insist on a rigidly abstract definition of comedy. No sooner does a comic genius appear—an Aristophanes, a Cervantes, a Molière—than he demolishes the theory, and in demolishing it he supplies the authentic pattern of comedy; organic, vital comedy genuinely sprung from human beings playing real parts in the world. For it is the function of comic genius to create values —values less exalted and less resplendent than those of other manifestations of poetic genius, but, it may be, the more precious for being more integrally bound up with our everyday existence.

It was long asserted that *Le Médecin Malgré Lui*— which, if it were called *Le Médecin Imaginaire*, would constitute a wonderful sequel to *Le Malade Imaginaire*—was put on in order to replenish a treasury depleted by *Le Misanthrope*. There is point in the contrast so drawn, but the La Grange account book sets the facts straight. *Le Médecin Malgré Lui* had its première on August 6, by which date *Le Misanthrope* had already been playing for some time. After twenty-one performances Alceste was on the point of having glutted the demand, as was natural enough. *Le Misanthrope*, when all is said, is not Molière's pre-eminent technical masterpiece. But it is a key work and a ripe work—one of those creations that, by threatening to disrupt the balance and harmony of an established form, bear witness to the mental stature of their creators.

SOCIETY TRIUMPHANT

"Molière, God of Laughter"

AT THE END of December 1666 Molière and his company were summoned to Saint Germain to arrange a new series of festivities. It was becoming more necessary than ever to humor the king—the future of *Tartuffe* depended on him—and to cater to his appetite for entertainment; for Molière was beginning to be alarmed by the mounting favor shown another Jean Baptiste—Lully, the obliging Florentine mogul of concert and dance. Molière the handy man of comedy was wearing by turns the moralist's garb and the mere entertainer's, as he was to do pending the time, now near, when he would decide on—or submit to—a costume half one thing and half the other.

It was decided to commemorate in an allegorical ballet the general supervision of art and literature that had been instituted by Colbert with Louis XIV's approbation. Mnemosyne, Mother of the Muses, was enjoined to appear and marvel at this great king who was not only heaping such distinctions on her daughters but was also supplying them with more dazzling themes than they had ever had access to before. Each Muse was honored with a special scene the subject of which conjured up her distinctive attributes. When it came Thalia's turn the actors of the royal company played the opening acts of *Mélicerte*, a heroic comedy on a subject that Molière had borrowed from *Le Grand Cyrus*—an instance of Comedy snatching its own from the custody of its victims. Otherwise, throughout these festivities, Molière was poking delightful fun at himself and his labors. *Mélicerte*, having served its purpose just as it was and having given the king pleasure, was left unfinished, to be superseded by a *Pastorale Comique* in which Molière made game of the sentimental rusticities of the genre. In this piece he was providing a very droll sort of burlesque of d'Estival, the finest basso in France.

With enjoyment abounding and the actors under instruction to spare no effort, the number of episodes performed exceeded the number of the Muses, and in late February Molière mounted a trifling play of his own invention, *Le Sicilien ou l'Amour Peintre*. It is an engaging work in which the author permits himself every liberty warranted by the conditions of production. The locale of the scenes shifts as in Shakespeare; the characterizations are deft; the diction is elevated. The works of this extemporized or unfinished sort, which Molière sowed broadcast at Saint Germain and Versailles, can be regarded as rough sketches in which every kind of new or newly resurrected technical device is tried out regardless of formula. Molière's imagination is prolific, and these sketches, slapped together with the airy impetuousness of a man making holiday, convey a notion—possibly an even more graphic one than *Don Juan*—of what Molière might have achieved in the Shakespearean mode. He received proper acknowledgment: his company's subvention was increased by 6000 livres. He had had his work cut out for him. Everyone had participated in this ballet in which the king himself was a dancer: the Spaniards of the company that was playing at the Hôtel de Bourgogne, the great actors in person, and even Lully—especially Lully, who had played the part of Orpheus and in it had duly delighted the audience.

The hero of *Mélicerte* was a young shepherd who, just then, was sowing distraction among society women of high degree. Molière had devised the part, and doubtless the whole play, for the glorification of a thirteen-year-old boy handsome as a god. For the lad this was a splendid stage debut. The young god had come within an eyelash of precipitating disaster. A box on the ear delivered by Armande had driven him out of Molière's house; he had declined to go back to it and had actually contemplated putting himself under the protection of none other than the king. Young Baron had no lack of self-assurance. Whether in sheer arrogance or in the calm assumption that everyone was fond of him, he well knew how to make people keep him in mind.

This youngster, destined to be the greatest tragic actor of the late seventeenth century, had not actually begun under Molière's auspices. His beauty, his winsomeness, and the fire of his acting, almost incredible in a child of twelve, had made him the star of the dauphin's small company, which was under the directorship of la Raisin. That great votary of love—she was ruining herself for the sake of one of the Prince of Monaco's officers—finding herself hard pressed in spite of the returns that Baron enabled her to count on, had gone to Molière and besought him to lend her his theater for three days. Molière, drawn by the young prodigy's fame, had had himself carried to the Palais Royal. (He was ill at the time.) After the performance he had taken Baron home with him, gazed at him interminably, and then had him given supper and a bed. One version will have it that the bed was Molière's own—whether that very night or later on is not specified. However one may elect to interpret the fact, it would appear that Molière, as long as he lived, regarded Baron with a fondness compounded of a father's affection, a teacher's pride, and a protective devotion of an indefinable sort. He was wretched when separated from Baron; he was dependent on him; he made him the companion of his solitude. And he indulged him in the outspokenness of the spoiled child; witness the episode recorded by Grimarest in which Baron outrageously browbeats Bernier the physician for being too smug about his travel experiences. Molière in the closing years of his life apparently hoped to get from Baron alone practically everything that he still expected from human beings.

I am well aware that it is possible to view the facts in a quite different light. Molière had lost his own son; he had only a daughter left; and here was a son come to him out of the blue—one fair as the dawn. Molière took pleasure in molding to the actor's profession such young persons as he was fond of. However impressive his success with Armande, it was far outshone by Baron, and that in the tragic mode, in which Molière himself was not greatly gifted. I am also well aware, however, that the striking parallel between Molière's present relationship with Baron and his former relationship with Armande exposes us to doubts, whether we want to harbor them or not. Proust might have been reminded in this connection of a concept that was important to him: the transference of an ill-starred love from one sex to the other. We seem to descry in Molière's make-up a need to combine love with domination, to gloat over the beloved person's step-by-step progress rather than over his ultimate success; a need to sustain and cleanse himself through the excellence of the guidance given; and, withal, a need for unjaded and glowing flesh to fondle, if but visually. Make allowance, too, for the jadedness of a sensual man of ripe years—a state conducive to transports over the whole category of youthful charms wrapped up in one flesh-and-blood parcel. But our information about the byways of Molière's emotional life is so inadequate that this tentative suggestion is no sooner formulated than it becomes lost in a blur. Transpose the foregoing into the key of friendship, without insisting on too exact a definition of its features, and you will be in no danger of going far wrong.

Molière was unable to perform *Le Sicilien* at the Palais Royal until the 10th of the following June. In the meantime he had had a serious relapse. During the struggle over *Tartuffe*, while Molière was intent on seizing the first available opportunity, his physician, Mauvilain, had decreed a rigid milk diet. It was certainly about this time that he rented lodgings in Auteuil, next to the Hôtel de Grou de Beaufort, at the intersection of the Rue de la Planchette and the Grand' Rue. For four hundred livres a year he also enjoyed the freedom of the Beaufort grounds. He was not giving up his residence in Paris: here was simply a place for withdrawal, relaxation, and reflection—a rural nook to which he came to breathe fresh air and drink milk from the neighboring farms. Well-to-do on an income of about 30,000 livres, he could allow himself the luxury of a few days' retirement and seclusion. When he went to Auteuil to rest, he was apparently seldom accompanied by Armande. Indeed, some kind of falling-out that tended to estrangement is commonly ascribed to just about this period. It may be that Molière, in keeping aloof from Armande—if he did—was keeping aloof from himself. Apparently his completion of *Le Misanthrope* slackened his bonds with life and left him apathetic to self-preservation.

In 1668, in fact, he composed and acted in three plays that combine an extraordinary inventiveness with a kind of brooding detachment. *Amphitryon* (January 13 at the Palais Royal), *George Dandin* (July 18 at Versailles), and *L'Avare* (September 9 at the Palais Royal) all exemplify, though in three very different ways, the return to comedy and the triumph of society, which is the triumph of the audience.

The comedy of *Amphitryon*, successfully played in Paris and Versailles until Easter and revived at Versailles when the court returned, is a comedy of pure entertainment. Molière had relaxed not at all since *L'École des Femmes*, and his extreme tenseness, increased by the agitations of his public career and of his private life, had reached the stage of actual cramp. He had identified himself more and more with his subjects; more and more he had put his own excitements and his own angers into his work, until the perspicacity proper to comedy was imperiled. His most recent comedies had been so close to life itself— I mean unconventionalized life in the raw—that they conveyed its harrowing disjointedness. Was his pres-

ent right-about-face a matter of conviction, or did the
professional man defer to the king's pleasure and the
public's?

Le Misanthrope demonstrated, but in a tormented
way, the triumph of the comic convention. Molière
had by no means ceased to believe in ridicule as a
universal touchstone. But he had learned that some
subjects are too far-reaching, that they unsettle the
convictions of audiences and consequently fail to attain the complete transparency that every art must
aspire to in its own province. The audience at a comedy needs to have a command of its subject matter—
to be neither too intimately challenged by it nor
plunged into doubts about its own beliefs. But we
see clearly only those matters whose actuality is not
brought into question.

The Greco-Roman comic tradition helped Molière
inestimably. We are ignorant, or virtually so, of how
the Romans looked on Jupiter's cuckolding of Amphitryon, but we do know that Louis XIV's French
people, inured to allegory, saw in it no more than an
engaging comic distraction. The comedy of *Amphitryon*, with its familiar cut-and-dried subject, its
graceful elegance, and its air of smiling over everything that it was making people laugh at, brought
back that atmosphere of tranquil relaxation, of elvish
unconcern for human stresses, in which the world
drifts before the audience's half-shut eyes with all
moorings cast off. The spectators were suddenly returned to the Garden of Epicurus. And Molière himself, virtually spared the necessity of inventing anything, thanks to Plautus and Rotrou, had had only to
put the play into verse and on to the stage. He had
performed the artist's function as divorced from the
moralist's; he had translated La Fontaine into theatrical
terms.

The free verse, a verse still rhymed but more flexible than the alexandrine—especially the alexandrine
as Molière handled it—allows for the succession of
light and shadow and accentuates the minutest details

of the action. The spoken word intimately matches the play of gesture and of mood; the variations in length of line unfailingly smooth the transition from shout to murmur, and rhythmic artifices capture in a tightly woven mesh of irony the intense emotions that are struggling to burst forth. *Amphitryon* is simply a fable of life size enacted by gilded shadows; and it is on a moral belonging rather to La Fontaine than to Molière that it closes, or rather dissolves.

The comic point of view is manifested in *Amphitryon* in its absolute state. That is to say, its function is not to prove anything or to reform anything; it comes into play strictly for its own sake. Dual vision, the quintessence of comedy, is the be-all and end-all of *Amphitryon*. These pairs of selves that mingle, separate, touch lightly on each other, and make us eye them so equivocally, embody the very ambiguity of laughter, or rather of smiling; and this is its own sufficient delight and asks nothing further. Be it noted, too, that impunity is no more chastised here than it is in *Tartuffe* or in *Don Juan*. But that circumstance no longer matters. I conceive that, for anyone with so importunate a disposition as Molière's and so overpowering a commitment to life, this casualness must have had a strong kinship to renunciation—a renunciation that shows the poet resurrected from the ashes of the man and resurveying his world from a remoter distance and a loftier height.

It was in the palace grounds at Versailles, in an auditorium framed in greenery, in which once more there was a blaze of gold and fountains were playing on every side, with the court and the papal nuncio in attendance, that the king's company staged *George Dandin*. Molière had resurrected his farce of long before, *La Jalousie de Barbouille*, on a theme out of Boccaccio. When we hear it said that *George Dandin* is the most implacable of Molière's comedies we observe that in it impunity is actually not chastised and that the ridiculous character is penalized pretty harshly for a shortcoming that, so far from being a crime, is hardly even a fault. George Dandin is quite literally a victim of the state of society. The artless and bland injustice wrought by the Sottenvilles is as remote as can be from the discernment under whose aegis the ridiculous figure, himself deserving, is overthrown. Society, exactly as it is, is victorious; and as society is, so everyone must be. We are here at a great remove from the identification of truth with the clear conscience and of depravity with error. The meaning of *George Dandin* is that if what is comic is to be based on *unquestioned* truth and error, it must relinquish equating these with moral values. What is left is a simple matter of accepting what is—of making terms with it how one will, or how one can. And that, beyond question, is an implacable enough lesson.

But do not overlook this point: The *form* of this comedy is a sufficient clue to what Molière meant by it. *George Dandin* is a farce, and its farcicality is no grinning mask pasted on a woebegone visage. It is conceived in such wise that its events come to pass far away from us and in another world—a world as aloof from us as that of *Amphitryon*. What is a farce if not a comic subject in the treatment of which the dramatic convention is illustrated by exaggerating, oversimplifying, or rigidifying the human theme? In *George Dandin* the wonderful truth of the picture is conveyed through the gestures and the voices of puppets. Every scene is a demonstration of some truism, as the invulnerability of the noble in his relation to the bourgeois, or the emptiness of the code of honor; but at the same time the caricature of the personae and of the principal motif deflects into laughter whatever emotions the subject matter might give rise to. Who are the readiest to make merry, and without the slightest disguise, over this lampoon of the nobility? Why, the nobles of the court circle, in whose eyes the Sottenvilles are primarily those provincials, those "country neighbors," at whom they never tire of scoffing. And George Dandin at the bolted door, George Dandin down on his knees, obtrudes on the audience a legendary image of mockery much more graphic and much more insistent than the injustice of his fate. The tints of comedy overlay everything and build up a glaze that utterly insulates the spectator from the essential humanity depicted. We have already observed this ambiguous comic art—or, better, this comic art raised to the second power—in *Les Précieuses Ridicules;* but here it takes on a different purport. It is no longer a simple tactical maneuver on Molière's part: it is a sanctuary or a carefully devised alibi. The artist is painting with firm strokes and as if with unconcern; the human being is no longer rebellious.

It is a suggestive fact and a seeming corroboration of these opinions that in *George Dandin* the comic motif of volition has turned into pure playfulness, as the comic motif of the dual image had turned into pure playfulness in *Amphitryon.* The bankruptcy of such a will as Arnolphe's or Alceste's constituted a drama, a crisis, and for the victim himself it was a disclosure that generated the action of the comedy; and a Sganarelle had no awareness of the juncture at which his will turned against himself. On the other hand George Dandin's "You asked for it!" is introduced from the very beginning as a stylized signal to notify the audience that the net is cast, the fish taken. And inasmuch as it is none other than the victim who proclaims the law of comedy, in an expressionless voice that is something short of human or has ceased to be human, his psalm of woe has a family resemblance to those ritualistic canticles that give voice to tribulations or to temperate rejoicings. Dandin as Molière portrays him portrays himself as an admittedly comic figure, without mirth to be sure, but also without protest; no doubt with no actual awareness of being comic, but with so unreserved an acceptance of a code infallibly tending to make him ridiculous that the human being is totally swallowed up in the dramatis persona.

George Dandin is among Molière's masterworks. It

was as well received in Paris as at Versailles. By the time it opened at the Palais Royal, in November, along with Subligny's *Folle Querelle*, a parody of *Andromaque*, *L'Avare* had already been playing for two months.

L'Avare is the least original of Molière's major works. There is hardly a scene in it, hardly one theatrical idea, that is not borrowed from Plautus, or from the structure of the *commedia dell' arte*, or from Ariosto or Larivey or Boisrobert. It is a comedy unadulterated, a caricature that is nothing but caricature, and it consummates Molière's surrender to his craft, his command of a system of conventionalized signals resembling musical motifs and calculated to exert a predetermined effect on the intelligence. The episodes of *L'Avare* are platitudes: Molière's whole endeavor was to turn them into axioms, and in this task of conversion he gave proof of a surpassing genius.

The function performed in *Amphitryon* by simple portraiture and in *George Dandin* by the will is here discharged by comic discernment. Every word, every gesture, every act of Harpagon is a searching depiction of his character, and the depiction is of a kind to turn the old man into something inhuman—a sort of beast of fable, in the category of chimeras or centaurs. We simultaneously accept him as real and reject him as preposterous, with the result that our minds, once the paroxysm of laughter is over, hold fast to nothing but the reality and discard the dehumanizing apparatus that has enabled the mind to grasp his reality. Harpagon, once we candidly accept the inherent difference between the theater and everyday life, is the logical end-product of Molière's system of character analysis applied to the comic protagonist. Cut off from his kind, deaf, blind, overwhelmed under his own fury, bombarding the world and unfailingly struck by every missile he launches, the comic protagonist in this play ends in insanity. Harpagon is a madman. We identify in him the lineaments of avarice precisely as in some types of lunatics we identify the lineaments of our will to power. Moreover his deeds are devoid of all human sequel except for the practical confusion that they produce. The celebrated scene of confrontation between father and son has made audiences shudder; but observe that Harpagon is not the least affected by it. All he perceives in it is an incentive to keep an even sharper eye on his son. He goes through the whole play in a state of hallucination, and inasmuch as he has recovered his cashbox he emerges virtually unscathed. If, like Goethe, we detect an element of the tragic in *L'Avare*, the proviso must be added that this element is instantly translated into comic terms. The cynicism of the portrait is corrected, or rather lightened, by the calculated and consistent excess of the colors applied. This abatement, however, is about the only one that can be cited. Extravagance of this sort is by definition outside reality. A madman can wreak no end of havoc, but he cannot continue doing it for long, and it is no great achievement on the part of society when it reasserts its authority over him. The retributive anger, the more refined punishment that is the outcome of an inward disharmony in the composition of a person like ourselves or closely resembling us, gives way here to the inevitable elimination of the person. Harpagon is sentenced in advance, as George Dandin is, and sentenced in the terms of theatrical justice, as the phantom figures of *Amphitryon* are.

Molière, when he had aspired to reform society, had brought the theater and the public closer together; he had engaged the auditor's interest in the plot as if it were something happening in his own house. Whether as a result of weariness or of disheartenment or of a return to the traditional canons of comedy, his most recent works bear witness to a different impulse. He is now minimizing the superficial correspondences between spectacle and spectator, and at the same time he is washing his hands of the moral implications of comedy. What we are

shown in *Amphitryon*, *George Dandin*, and *L'Avare*
is no longer the middle-class world of the earliest
great plays, with its mingled sordidness and generosity, nor yet is it the frivolous, carefree world of
L'Étourdi, of *Le Dépit Amoureux*, or of *Sganarelle*:
rather, it is a world of cynical aloofness, unconcerned
with good and evil. And it is by means of an artifice
that the extravagance of the portraiture absolves us
from feeling indignation. Histrionic caricature pro-
vides the beholder with a screen behind which he may
laugh unembarrassed, surveying what goes on as from
olympian heights. This effect is striking in *Monsieur
de Pourceaugnac*, received with plaudits at Chambord
in October 1669—a farce nearer than Molière's preceding works to the Latin and the Italian comic pattern. It is about two schemers who gloat over having
robbed fellow creatures or got them hanged. In it an
apothecary is delighted because the physician he
recommends has killed three children, none other than
his own. The protagonist who is made a fool of
scarcely justifies his victim's role. The crime committed by Monsieur de Pourceaugnac—who is hardly
more worthless than the dubious lovers by whom he
is gulled—is essentially the crime of being a bumpkin.
This farce plays fast and loose with plausibility. Having not the smallest pretension to anything beyond
diverting us with droll predicaments, it picks out
whatever predicaments it has a fancy for, undeterred
by any risk of prejudicing our comfortable assump-
tions. Here is the reason why farce can be more
unsparing, more pitiless, than comedy: it eschews all
pretension to being taken seriously.

Monsieur de Pourceaugnac was a hit both at the
court and in the city—a seeming proof that it was not
the basic theme of *L'Avare* that had been found repellent. We know that the last-named comedy, after a
middling initial success, was thereafter no more than
semipopular, despite rather frequent performances.
Contemporary audiences are said not to have approved
the idea of a comedy of major pretensions written in

prose. The sluggishness and stiffness of the preliminary exposition were disconcerting, especially as coming from the author of *Tartuffe*. And—a decisive point—*Monsieur de Pourceaugnac*, like *George Dandin* and in contrast with *L'Avare*, was put into a framework of ballet. The inburst of apothecaries alone would have ensured the success of the piece. Legend has it that at one performance of the farce Lully, clowning it along with the rest, hurled himself on a harpsichord and reduced it to splinters, to the vast enjoyment of Louis XIV. Molière playing Pourceaugnac, a stupendous butt of laughter in his blue velvet jerkin, green garters, hat with green plume, and green taffeta sash, must, I conceive, have dazed the beholders as a clown dazes us. The mere sight of him was a license for any excess.

Ballet was acquiring at the court a more and more important rank among forms of amusement. Steadily fashionable from the sixteenth century, it was tending to become the pre-eminent type of spectacle and to impose its own unity on the other forms of public entertainment. In the *Gazette* Molière's comedy ballets, including even *Le Bourgeois Gentilhomme*, are scarcely mentioned except as ancillary to dance and song—as components of a more lavish whole more adequately expressive of the royal renown. Ballet under Louis XIV is a relaxation of war—war holding the mirror up to itself. Military evolutions, passados, and feats of heroism are prolonged and freed in the motions of the dance; and in them, too, the thirst for power and the thirst for luxury exuberate in realistic sensuous detail that makes a sharp contrast with the poetic bent of the period. Liberties denied elsewhere are taken in ballet. Indirections, subtleties, and all the modesties are dismissed from it. Whatever is the most literal, insistent, detailed, and sumptuous brings the greatest applause. There is hardly any kind of artisan that is not needed as a contributor to the general effect, in which mechanical rather than poetic achievements cause the tide to turn or boulders to take wing or gods to be made slaves to the amusement of mortals. The supernatural, evicted from the higher arts, is triumphant here. But it is triumphant at a cost to itself, for it is made materialistic, merged with stage props and mechanical contraptions, rendered completely palpable, and thereby stripped of any poetic quality. When, later, a Voltaire displays an equal insensitiveness to the poetry of the supernatural, what he has to thank for it may be that successor to the ballet, the opera.

The *Divertissement Royal*, presented at Saint Germain in 1670, marks the high point of this order of composition. The king, fortunate in war and fortunate in love, had conceived the notion of telescoping all the most breath-taking effects jointly producible by mechanical and human resources. On this system every one of his ballets was a minor campaign that he conducted between his major ones and directed with his characteristic appetite for power and for wreckage. He propounded to Molière for an ostensible subject the rivalry of two princes who stage a battle of competitive splendor over which shall sweep a princess off her feet. Molière conjured up a third despoiler, a gallant general of inferior station who captures the favor of Ériphyle and weds her by means of a stratagem not devised for her. The time was that of Mademoiselle d'Orléans's infatuation with Lauzun, and the princess herself was present at the performance. In it she could read the warnings of a comedy that ended by humoring her vagary. In it, too, Molière adumbrated a fairly telling lampoon of astrology. The plot is unraveled by the apparition of Venus; but the *dea ex machina* is served by what is also a mechanical contrivance within the play itself, rigged by the astrologer to serve the purpose of one of the princes. By such means the world is hermetically sealed; the means of exit provided for us are but dummy windows.

Molière, acting in *Les Amants Magnifiques*, played a clownish psychologizer who might have been his twin. Disillusioned yet not at all pessimistic, surveying mankind as a congeries of mechanisms neither more nor less miraculous than the imitation boulders and gilded cardboard gods of the stage, he paralleled the backstage mechanicians by pressing as called for on the springs of human motive. The mechanistic psychology of a Marivaux evinces itself here in sharp definition, already aglitter with the sensual polish in which the eighteenth century specialized. We find Molière dallying, too, with shrewdly measured proportions of discretion and of temerity in sundry retorts and asides that convey, as it seems to me, a good idea of his current status at court. "Hush!" Clitidas admonishes himself; "don't you realize that astrology is a government matter and that you mustn't harp on that string? I've told you any number of times you make too free and help yourself to various liberties that are going to get you into trouble." This part of Clitidas may denote a degree of change in Molière— a diminution of intensity and aggressiveness, an increase in imperturbability and readiness to spare his victim; an increase in irony, rooted in acceptance of the world as it is and prevailing over satire, which refuses to accept it; an increase in weariness and, it may be, a modicum of reasoned renunciation.

In what frame of mind Molière accepted the competition of mechanical apparatus and music, we do not know; opinions vary, matching the temperaments behind them. In one scene of *Le Bourgeois Gentilhomme* this comedy, the last word in ballet spectacle, derides the purveyors of ballet spectacle. But Molière must have felt some apprehension. He had a rival, and one more dangerous than any vogue, because he was a creator of vogues; a rival who was younger and more hale. The two Jean Baptistes at once constituted a form of dual vision that was not funny to him. Molière respected Lully; but how could he fail to fear this man of fierce ambition who worked with demoniacal energy and stopped at nothing, whether committing assault and battery on a harpsichord or cajoling the most ravishing cadences from it or mak-

ing himself simper from head to foot as if soliciting an
appointment as secretary to the king? Lully the omnipresent, omnifacient Chiacherone was Comedy per-
sonified, yet tempered to the current taste; he was a
ropedancer who had won a genuine patent of nobility; he was an inhibitionless Molière of a suppleness
perpetually proof against arthritis. He had the king's
smiles, the king's congratulations. Molière, already ill
and shortly to be dying, was no longer unique, and
he therefore felt himself to be no longer indispensable.

Nevertheless he carried on courageously. The men
of that epoch were builders and planners. Ministers
of the crown, conquerors of cities, writers of plays
—each of them followed his own path as far as his
abilities would take him, and each was sharer in a
total reality transcending himself. Molière is a servant
just as a Vauban is, and the service that he gives is
matchless. Whether he has wanted or not wanted his
servitude to the ballet, he strives to get the best out
of it that he can. And that best is wonderful. Ballet
offered comedy the great boon of providing it with
innumerable exits. It was enabled to steal away, return,
intermit, resume, all at its own pleasure. There was no
need, before the comic action dissolved into a ballet
routine as a set piece of fireworks bursts into flower,
to devise for it an ending conformed to rule: the plot
literally unraveled itself by becoming swallowed up in
a masquerade. The denouement in legitimate comedy
was a difficult problem, because it was required to
provide a plausible solution to a story that was itself
not too plausible—to bring back into the domain of
reality a representation that had been carried to unreal lengths. Ballet is to comedy what death is to
tragedy: a leap into the beyond, the rounding of an
orbit, a flight ending only at the ultimate goal, with
no return and no artificial compromise with mundane
perspective. The abeyance of distinction between
comedy and ballet, together with the audience's ad-
justment to seeing dramatic terms translated into

choreographic and musical terms, enables the author to accomplish the most complete transposition of his reading of life into the theatrical key. This Molière did, and did superlatively.

A Turk named Suleiman, a rather insignificant person, had visited Paris and the court. The king, by way of dazzling him, had loaded himself with diamonds. The Turk had merely turned up his nose: he had seen diamonds in plenty in his own country. For some time after that there was a rage for anything Turkish. The Chevalier d'Arvieux, who had done duty as Suleiman's interpreter, set Louis XIV and Madame de Montespan laughing by spinning them yarns about his travels in the East. It occurred to the king that a Turkish ceremonial would make an extremely fetching ballet. He enjoined d'Arvieux to consult with the two Jean Baptistes with a view to organizing this divertissement. The Chevalier went to Auteuil to join Molière; the three men set to work; and so there came into being *Le Bourgeois Gentilhomme*.

The ballet was put on at Chambord in October 1670. First there was a big-game hunt, and then came the pursuit of absurdity, which was much more expensive: the divertissement cost, all told, not less than 49,000 livres. We have the famous and familiar anecdote in which, the king not saying a word after the performance, the courtiers fall to carping at the play and asserting that Molière has deteriorated sadly; then, after the second performance, Louis XIV assures Molière that he has never done anything finer. Without being overcredulous as far as the anecdote is concerned, we may compliment the king on his discrimination. Molière had seldom surpassed this wondrous work. And this time his success was proportionate to his merit. Played at the Palais Royal from November 23, *Le Bourgeois Gentilhomme* collected enormous receipts. To be sure, it was performed along with the entire divertissement, and Molière was not the only beneficiary of its triumph. The king had profusely congratulated Lully, who had outdone even himself in his impersonation of the Mufti in the Turkish ceremonial.

Le Bourgeois Gentilhomme is one of those works in which an author's various gifts achieve ideal balance. Made game of as Pourceaugnac is, Monsieur Jourdain is a butt by reason of his personality, unlike the man of Limoges, and to see him gulled does not distress us. Like Harpagon, he is a madman, but a sprightly madman, a joyous madman. Whereas avarice narrows, hardens, and bedarkens, vanity relieves its creature of every earthly burden. The acid of comedy measured out by Molière hardens the feelings, but that is because feelings are what they are; for the portraiture is truthful all the way. The ridiculous extreme of vanity tends to produce the effect of its opposite, and that just in proportion to the insistence of the portraiture. Molière is able to bear down with all his weight without danger of going wrong; and that is why *Le Bourgeois Gentilhomme*, which is comic throughout, is also entertaining throughout.

No pains are taken to make the story plausible. The relaxation is complete; the only foresight needed is that proper to all comedy of serious pretensions. But relaxation, in Molière, does not at all mean incoherence. Disencumbered of realism, he is preoccupied only with truth. Every scene of *Le Bourgeois Gentil-homme* is a wonderfully accurate and sprightly demonstration of some theorem of personality or of feeling, reduced to the fewest and simplest lines. And these lines are made perceptible by various pieces of stage business that usher in the ballet routines. It is all extraordinarily pellucid; the sense of it reaches us directly through our own senses, without verbiage.

Le Bourgeois Gentilhomme signalizes the triumph of society. Molière's typical comic character defends himself from his own kind by a futile defiance of society. Monsieur Jourdain does the opposite. He has a wholehearted social ambition. Above the level of commoners there is a whole separate world—a world of sights, sounds, concepts, graces, distinctions. Monsieur Jourdain confronting this world is as a child and, at the same time, as a foreigner. He murders its speech with his ludicrous pronunciation, but at the same time he works hard at it with the contortions of a newborn baby. A foreigner willy-nilly, he has an absurdity that is redeemed by the freshness brought to flower. Monsieur Jourdain is perpetually ecstatic over everything that is making him ridiculous. Monsieur Jourdain is not unhappy. Monsieur Jourdain wants to be a conformer. We do not hold it against him; we feel protective toward him; we are a bit fond of him. When the hunt closes in on him at last, we find that we want him spared.

On either flank of Monsieur Jourdain, in the foreground but slightly drawn back, we have those two unforgettable creations, Dorante and Madame Jourdain. Dorante is a moderated version of Don Juan, resorting to shifty practices in order to pay Monsieur Dimanche. Since his invulnerabilities are offset by his necessities, he has become an essentially comic figure, even though he continues to pull the strings himself. Already, thus early, a foreshadower of the eighteenth century, he is scarcely a force at all any more in his own day, though the time is at hand when he will have become a recognizable type. But how easygoing and clear-cut his speech still is, how charged with a bland insolence! Molière, by a wonderful kind of psychic musicianship, preserves for us the very inflection of dead-and-gone voices in comedies that count for more than whole libraries of speech recordings. Leaf through *Le Bourgeois Gentilhomme* and listen to Madame Jourdain's utterances—curt, pithy sayings that combine suggestions of song and of proverb. This solid housewife, fists on hips, takes one step back whenever her husband takes one forward. In her characteristic sayings she proclaims, while Monsieur Jourdain is stammering out his courtly speeches, her kinship with the folk. It is a curious fact that neither uses the diction of their social class. Their middle-class status is a sort of string on which one of them plays in a high register, the other in a low. *Le Bourgeois Gentilhomme* makes us privy to the very forces that actuate society, shown us under the guise of a domestic quarrel. And that statement is no mere figure of speech.

One fairy failed to attend the birth of Monsieur Jourdain: the one that had inspired *Tartuffe* and *Le Misanthrope*. But *Le Bourgeois Gentilhomme*, accepted for what it is, maintains its place among comic creations of the first order. As a masterpiece of relaxed ease and of sheer entertainment, it makes a worthy companion to that masterpiece of tension, *L'École des Femmes*. Molière, in the two years of life that remained to him, was to reach the same height again, but never a higher. He is now the absolute master of his craft—one equaled in nicety and firmness by hardly any that we know.

In the course of his career, as a by-product of miscellaneous controversies, he codified or got codified the philosophy of that craft. It consists of but two bold concepts. One of them is the ridiculous; the other is stagecraft. Molière's stroke of genius was to weld the two together into one seamless whole. Any ridiculous occurrence is a dramatic occurrence; any piece of stage business is an ethical analysis. Inasmuch as the ridiculous is simultaneously a facet of truth and a piece of stage business, it is comedy that constitutes the ideal stage vehicle for the representation of human beings.

The ridiculous is a facet of truth; it is truth made palpable. In the *Lettre sur la Comédie de l'Imposteur* it is set down that Comedy is "the outward and palpable shape that a provision of nature has stamped on everything irrational." No statement could be clearer. When we laugh we are detecting error through the agency of no abstract idea, but embodied in direct sensory communications, some of them actually to the muscles. Laughter is evocation of the rational faculty.

But how achieve the dual vision that brings out

what is funny—the mandate of the rational faculty, the judicial faculty? Take a simple example of a bystander spotting an inconsistency in one of his fellows. Say that he hears this man quote and extol Seneca on the subject of anger one day, and the next day sees him fly into a rage. It is the accumulation of just such data that constitutes our knowledge of people. These inconsistencies of behavior, if scattered far apart in time and thrown out of connection with one another by the incoherence of daily living, lose much of the pungency of their contrast. But if our bystander remembers, if he blends his two observations into one thought process so that the inconsistency is brought out and rendered ludicrous, that is enough, for it gives him two mutually incompatible pictures of the same person. Remembering, he passes a judgment, and it is this judgment that embodies the ridiculousness of the observed behavior. It is, then, imperative, if ridiculousness is to be made graphic, that the bystander make his own judgment graphic as such, giving it the appropriate logical shape. He will juxtapose, one after the other, his philosopher's pompous theoretical manifesto against anger and his fit of rage, that the two occurrences may be as intimately connected in fact as they are in his recollection of them. But even thus much is not enough. He will establish a still more intimate bond—a logical one—between the abstract disapproval of anger and the anger itself. The philosopher shall lose his temper because someone mocks at his calling, which includes teaching people to mock at loss of temper. And there you have all the components of the comic occurrence superposed: first a preparation of the ground that enlists our interest and gives the occurrence actuality —to wit, the philosopher's stuffy proclamation of his doctrine—and then the ludicrous tantrum that touches off the avalanche of laughter. The net result is the philosophy preceptor's scene in *Le Bourgeois Gentilhomme*. Be it noted that this scene is a projection of the judgment made by the bystander. The ridiculous

sequence from cause to effect is a mental process introduced into the actual occurrence in order to give
it, so to say, the stamp of rationality.

But this judgment-brought-to-life is also inherently
a plot—a dramatic plot with characters expressly
adapted to stage perspective. The thought process,
when it collects into one bundle of reasoned absurdity
the various attitudes of a given person, will have
composed by the same stroke a dramatic sequence.
The creative plot is not merely a faithful transcription
of probability. It owes its roundedness, its impact,
and its interest to its *meaning*—to the moral pene-
tration that it manifests. But a dramatic plot is by no
means sustained, as the plot of a novel is, by dint of
analysis and narrative license. It derives its meaning
and its scope from no source but itself. It is under a
necessity of being self-explanatory at the very moment of its unfolding. The dramatization of a judgment—one that excites laughter for understood reasons
—is therefore the quintessence of good theater.

Molière applied this formula to his depiction of
characters and of emotions. His art is the reproduc-
tion of reality with criticism added; in it the meaning
of the acts performed is immediately conveyed to us,
with the true and the false utterly transparent. The
chapter "Faux Raisonnements" of the Port Royal
Logique is adapted to and carried over to the theater.
We must be careful, though, to avoid confusing
Molière with those manufacturers of machine-made
lay figures who use the stage to show us simplified
illustrations of their general ideas. Molière's personae,
as far as their bearing on truth and falsity is concerned, are no object lessons. They are living creatures who forced themselves on Molière—as we saw
in considering *Les Fâcheux*—with the violence of a
collision. And his bringing them under judgment,
which is synonymous with his bringing them on to
the stage, is as an act of retaliation by a hounded man.
Molière's characters are part and parcel of Molière's
life—a succession of figures that he furbished for pur-

poses of attack or of defense. Whence the atmosphere of actuality that gives comedy its crowning touch. Bergson makes the searching observation that the most trivial saying with wit in it is the raw material of a stage scene; and he is right. Watch a consciously funny man. He never gives the effect of arranging his features into an expression: it is as if his features took him by surprise. The subterfuge is indispensable. The entire comic effect ensues, when all is said, from the mental pasquinade that consists in putting on a disguise of reality to provide an alibi the unmasking of which will command laughter. But there is no comedy of stature save as the author has experienced being taken unaware in his own person, has seen with his own eyes the element of caricature inherent in human affairs, and has had, if but fleetingly, the illusion that the alibi was real.

All these observations boil down to the statement —if only we can agree on the meaning of the words used—that Molière is first of all a stupendous master of stagecraft. We know that he seized upon his own wherever he found it. What engages him is not the subject matter, the theme, but rather the interplay of personalities and of stage effects. In that mathematics-minded period only relationships mattered. A reused theme, if compressed, given a new focus, and made transparent, seemed more original than a freshly invented structure of ideas or even of language. The audience, so far from being blasé, delighted in re-experiencing traditional witticisms and antics brought to a new perfection, and devices and effects were the better received for being familiar. Aristophanes, the Latin authors, the writers of fabliaux and farces, the French and Italian tellers of tales—Rabelais, Boccaccio, Cervantes—constituted an inexhaustible storehouse and sometimes a priceless testing ground. Molière schooled himself as any fine technician must: alert memory, the books at his disposal, the master habit of mind—these took care of his subject, leaving His significant work began at the point of tran his subject matter to the stage. From that point on, playwright, manager, and actor were as one. A first consideration was to supply each of the players with a part adapted to his gifts, his build, his peculiarities, and the impression of himself that he had given Molière. The casting was an integral process in the creation of the play, and Molière's absolute authority over his associates made the arrangement of his cast of characters an easy matter. Theatrical ideas, as we have seen, are only critical ideas brought into focus.

But it is not enough to pass these ideas on to the audience in their raw state. Stage action must not only be self-explanatory while it is unfolding: over and above that it must make itself moving to the beholders —must, if I may venture to say so, be compelling. It is often said that dramatic works, having but little time at their disposal, must get their effects by over-emphasis; but that is only a half-truth. If we take it into account that any play repeats the same effects a good many times, we shall discover that the drama has much more time at its disposal than we realize. What is required is that the stage effect be completely discharged—consummated at the first attempt, without any faltering or stumbling; but once it is discharged it has to be repeated and in a sense made to double back on itself in order that, as the phrase is, it may get across the footlights. The knack of repetition is one of the secrets of Molière's genius.

Consider Cléante's well-known harangue:

> The truly pious, heirs to heaven's grace,
> Do not put on a sanctimonious face.
> Come now, cannot you tell apart
> The hypocrite and him of contrite heart?
> Would you approve them both in equal phrases,
> Give face and hollow mask the selfsame praises,
> Treat subterfuge and trickery as though
> The inward truth were one with outward show,
> Accept a shadow for reality
> \nd bogus coins for honest currency?

Some commentators have perceived in this repetitive effect an evidence of Molière's conscientiousness—his insistence on expressing himself unmistakably on a subtle point. He merely wanted to express himself, to make his meaning clear, through a device shared by oratory and drama.

If you remember the irresistible balcony scene in *L'École des Femmes*, you will find it amusing to look up the earliest outline of it, or one of the earliest, in Scarron's tale *La Précaution Inutile*: "So saying, the two gentlemen made each a deep bow to the Spanish lady, at the cost of some slight difficulty in accomplishing it with credit. Dom Pèdre in particular executed his bow against such a protest from his whole body as made him think he had sprained his back. The lady of the balcony made them a curtsy of sorts; whereupon Dom Pèdre and his companion mustered the fortitude for two more bows." Out of this passage Molière salvages the business hinted in the self-multiplying bows and uses it to start up his repeating apparatus:

> . . . A fine young man who, when our glances cross,
> Sweeps me a bow with not an instant's loss.
> I, not to be outdone in courtesy,
> Show him that I can bow as low as he.
> Promptly a second time he now bows low;
> Likewise do I with all punctilio.
> Again behold him from the waist inclined;
> And for the third time I retort in kind.

A great many passages of dialogue in Molière consist of just such repetitions in ingeniously varied patterns calculated to imprint dramatic motifs on the audience's memory. Such is the function of the many recurrences of "It is true that . . . ," "That is obvious," "It could not be better put"—phrases that reinforce the repetitions extracted from the second speaker and serve him as springboards.

For an effect is made to wax in the process of repetition. There is more to it at the end than at the beginning. When, in the celebrated "poor man" scene, Dorine tells Orgon that she is going to apprise Elmire of his share in his wife's illness, Orgon's character has been fathomed in the interchanges just preceding, each to the last more telling than the one before. Almost invariably the character or the meaning to be fathomed is comparatively static; that is to say, it is determined once for all and undergoes no development, so that to repeat is only to reaffirm it; but repetition has the effect of a magnifying glass that renders the object fully and inescapably visible. The system of comic analysis is enhanced by the rhythm of the dialogue, which, though broken into units of extremely variable length, is always homogeneous in that its exchanges parcel out the central idea just as in a ballet the successive movements parcel out the component parts of the subject. Agnès's outburst, for example, is a dialogue of verbal curtsies. Molière's art consists here in gauging, with the stage manager's inner ear, the precise duration of each rhythmic evolution. One of Molière's scenes is at the same time a demonstration and a dance.

An unerring judicial faculty, simplified but the more stageworthy for that; an art of dramatic composition as austere as the judicial faculty itself; propitious attitudes in an audience satisfied with beings of little complexity depicted in terms of its own primary characteristics—these are the extricable ingredients of Molière's practice. The rest of it defies analysis. Molière is a superlative mimic, not only of basic characters or what we call "things in general," but also of the individuals he encounters—of what at bottom actuates them and of their impalpable uniqueness. And he is master not only of the individual as he is, but also of his past. Mimicry of Molière's kind emphatically does not mean a creation of types—persons who stand for a numerous contemporary class: rather it means making palpable in a person the preceding generations that shaped him—giving him a voice that is a composite of all the voices ever heard in his story.

Madame Jourdain's apothegms are symbolic. The whole meaning and the whole sound of Molière's give-and-take have a proverbial cast. The making of a Molière takes a good deal more than innate critical and dramatic genius. It takes a folk tradition, to be concentrated in every word spoken, every gesture improvised. And it is here that his art laughs at attempts to define it; it is here that his art, logical as it is, captures the baffling actuality of life unadulterated.

One thing that we shall never know—and how we should love to know it!—is whether Molière had vanity enough to revel in his own genius. When he was putting outbursts so inspired into the mouths of Harpagon and Argan, for the one about his money, for the other about his belly; when he was making so much of little Louison; when he was bringing into focus a piece of stage business in which he was welding into one the realism of a plot and the substance of a lucid meaning—was he being oblivious of Armande and Lully, of his own disease and the lamentable visage of reality? Tradition gives us no encouragement to hope so. The Molière of 1670 as we have him in the accounts of his friends—and, not too distortedly, in those of his enemies in *L'Élomire Hypocondre*—is the Molière of Auteuil, at many points resembling him whom we already know: a man of reflection, of alternation between melancholy and gusto—a silent man of a serene but penetrating wisdom. But if he has little to say, he daily coughs more. The energetic workman is sapped of his strength; he is as if depleted by his malady.

It was about this time that Baron came back to him to play the part of Amour in *Psyché*. Psyché herself was Armande, costumed in cloth of gold and lace and fine silver. We are free to make our own guess whether this duetto, with its graces and Baron's handsomeness and their mincing murmured endearments, occasioned gossip. The event took place in the great hall of machinery in the Tuileries, early in 1671. Corneille, who had written the greater part of the piece, was himself not impervious to the charms of "Mademoiselle Molière." It is not without a touch of deferential irony that we contemplate Corneille returned to the Palais Royal. This reconciliation was a logical sequel to the falling out between Molière and Racine. The secular world's affairs work out after the pattern of stage comedy. Tragedy in the pattern of Corneille was alien to Molière's gifts, and he never made the most of its finest effects, anyway. Of *Attila*, *Tite*, and *Bérénice* acted on a stage dedicated to comedy, the less said the better. In any event the creator of *Cinna* so far regained his singularly artless gusto as to celebrate in delightful verse the jealousies and bewilderments of first love.

Baron was no man to reject any stroke of luck. We have to conclude either that the tender feelings attributed to Armande are a figment or else that Molière was experiencing that moral apathy that exculpates others of one's worries and jealousies. For the quondam shepherd, now grown up, never parted again from his preceptor until death separated them. Molière even appears to have laid himself out to set Baron some fine examples of practical everyday benevolence. On one occasion he heaped kindnesses on the aged actor Mondorge and made Baron a partner in his well-doing. Again, when Boileau, La Fontaine, and Chapelle set out to drown themselves after some inordinate drinking, Molière prevailed on them to put it off until the next day, using the argument that such matters ought to be dealt with in a state of self-possession and complete awareness of the issue—an argument that combines a good act with an engaging mockery of the human will. Molière plays host to Bernier, to other friends, to strangers. People go to see him; they love conversing with him, getting his advice. His counsel on practical affairs has come to be as uncompromising as if documented with lawbooks. A sort of counselor of the affections and of behavior—so Molière appears to us to be as he nears the end.

And meanwhile he was plying his trade as ever. The Palais Royal was undergoing radical alterations. Its interior was being done over to accommodate improved mechanical facilities; it was desired to present *Psyché* there with all the new equipment. Between July 24 and October 25 the performances of this comedy ballet brought in 33,000 livres. The play delighted the city. Among innovations worth mentioning, be it noted that the so-called musicians sang while mingled with the actors, and did it unmasked. Hitherto they had insisted on being out of sight, enclosed in stage boxes behind grilles, to preserve their distance.

On May 24, while the theater was being remodeled, Molière had put on, with but moderate success, a farce derived from Terence. *Les Fourberies de Scapin* displays throughout a Molière preoccupied with Latin comedy and Gallic farce, doubtless because he lacked the time to work out a theme after his characteristic pattern, but possibly, too, because just then he was feeling more confident of achieving his effects by utilizing time-honored ones.

On December 1, 1671 the new Duchesse d'Orléans, successor to Molière's amiable patroness, was welcomed to Saint Germain. The king wanted to present her with the performance of a grandiose ballet made up of the finest parts of earlier ones. Molière wove into it a *Pastorale* and, as was his wont, a comedy. *La Comtesse d'Escarbagnac* is a rough sketch—a sort of Balzacian pencil drawing that foreshadows, more distinctly than even Dorante does in *Le Bourgeois Gentilhomme*, the cynical eighteenth-century comedy. It is a work that represents Molière the pure painter and mimic—a Molière who assumes not the smallest responsibility for the society that he caricatures. The actors, after staying at Saint Germain to December 7, returned to their own Palais Royal on February 9. On the 17th Molière missed playing his parts in the current divertissement, the *Ballet des Ballets:* he had

been suddenly recalled to Paris. For there Madeleine
Béjart had just died.

She had had time to arrange her affairs. She had had
a priest summoned. She had experienced the full measure of repentance that was customary for the period,
particularly among stage folk; it might almost be
called routine. Also, she had made provision for masses
in perpetuum. Molière followed her body to Saint
Germain l'Auxerrois and then to Saint Paul's, where
Madeleine had asked that she be buried. What were
Molière's reflections, mental pictures, and memories
on the way, we can guess with no great difficulty;
but we forgo this perfect opportunity for some in-
expensive fictioneering. Be it remembered only that a
man gravely ill—a dying man—was following a dead
woman, and that this dead woman had had almost as
integral a share in his public career and in the most
intimate parts of his private life as he had had himself.

Shortly before Madeleine's death Molière had as-
signed parts for *Les Femmes Savantes*. He had been
granted a license for the play near the end of 1670; his
planning of the play may have dated from 1668. Two
days before the première Molière in a public an-
nouncement admonished audiences not to find in *Les
Femmes Savantes* any personal attacks on his contemporaries—a beguiling way of stirring up public curiosity. The receipts, especially at the outset, were grati-
fying; the première brought in 1735 livres. There was
vast enjoyment of two poems by Abbé Cotin, delivered in all their coarseness by Trissotin; also of the
stage spectacle made of the notorious fight that had
Cotin and Ménage at each other's throats at the house
of Mademoiselle de Montpensier. The powerfully
rhythmical lines of the play had a more than ordinary
impact, and there was gratification over Molière's
return to his earlier manner—a felicitous blending of
the spiritedness of *Les Précieuses Ridicules* with the
polished versification of *Tartuffe*.

Molière in *Les Femmes Savantes* reaffirms the unity
of truth with goodness, of falsity with evil—an idea

that he cherished, though his clear-sightedness, and also his weariness, were continually disrupting it or threatening to do so. This time he had one of those entirely noncommittal themes that permit an author, without insincerity, to indulge the audience's distaste for being morally upset. Here we are at a great remove from the tense and thorny humor of *L'École des Femmes*, the bold thrusts of *Tartuffe* and *Don Juan*, the equivocal purport of *Le Misanthrope;* but for all that we are in the domain of high comedy. The play is put together as *Tartuffe* is, with a comfortable middle-class interior, an atmosphere of reality that brings the stage close to the audience, a ruling extravagance of current fashion taken advantage of by a schemer, and eventual triumph of rectitude and common sense. But the intrigue is made gentler, less unsparing. Learning plays here the part played by religion in *Tartuffe* and by love in *L'École des Femmes*. It is a less ponderous, less austere subject, a more unassuming one; and Trissotin's impunity never gives us the shudders. To measure how far apart this play is from its predecessors we need only inquire why the contrivance that unravels the plot would have been, in *Tartuffe*, unthinkable.

Les Femmes Savantes has two themes, interwoven but easily enough picked apart. Both are derived from *Les Précieuses Ridicules*, and both are given new depth. The first is a resumption of the aggressive by the male as nature made him, with whom first the Précieuses and now the Savantes refuse to cohabit. This was one of Molière's cherished themes: his own make-up kept him chronically exasperated on the subject. The indictment in the play is a stern one. The three learned ladies are belabored tirelessly and unsparingly, and Armande most of all. We should call her nowadays an instance of defective sublimation. She will consent neither to put herself to any expense for heaven's sake nor to sacrifice any of her mundane advantages. Moreover, she is not harebrained as her mother and her sister are, and, incessantly chastened

not only by outsiders but also by Henriette and Clitandre, she is compelled to be aware of it and to endure it. It is to this sort of retribution, rather than to
the sententious speeches, that we must look for Molière's moral lesson. The lesson is one accepted, it has
been said, by all decent folk—nature's own lesson.
Maybe so; but it is first of all the lesson of truth.
Molière is one of those exceptional beings—exceptional in any age—who are provoked by error. We
have seen that trouble began for him at the point at
which society, his partner in creation, completely
failed to detect error where he detected it, or where
he himself fell short of a clear perception of it. But
in this play the audience's conscience and his own
indignation coincided, enhancing his picture and giving it brilliance. The characterization of Armande is
a signal example of how a rather subtle personality can
be depicted on the stage in bold and simple strokes.

The second theme of *Les Femmes Savantes* is the
literary life seen satirically. Moliére, with admirable
perceptiveness, refrained from making it his central
subject. The writer is a poor topic for comedy: he has
to be taken to task in connection with the aberrations
of literary society or, better yet, with his influence on
fools. *Les Femmes Savantes* is a satire on the salon—
the comedy of the salon self-perceived and self-
judged. It has been said that the salon depicted is, thus
early, an eighteenth-century coterie. It seems to me
that the salons of every period exhibit the same absurdities—inflated importance bestowed on the "intel-
lectuals" who lay down the law, morbid appetite for
culture in the feminine participants, and loss of the
sense of proportion. Molière is squaring accounts with
a history filled with altercations, and above all he is
doing retaliatory justice to comedy and the comic
actor—a literary retaliation of a cogency not to be
withstood. Comedy has won its prerogatives, and now
it is simply making them count.

Molière, when he made the Précieuses' father Philaminte's husband, converted a social satire into a com-

edy of manners. Philaminte's aberration is of a specialized kind: it is the aberration of a woman called on
to discharge the functions of her husband, perhaps not
so much by her own inclination as by his chronic
incapacity. Here is an instance of social imbalance that
has repercussions on morale and disrupts it. The play
is not so much the comedy of learned ladies as it is
the comedy of women without men. A scintillating
work superbly written, it is Molière's testament in the
comic mode. Poetic quality and insight count for less
in it than in some others of his comedies; it is more
than a little talky, and the speeches are not Molière's
best; but for that very reason it is clearer, and of all
his works it is the one that has yielded the greatest
number of aphorisms.

Molière is criticized for letting his humanism rest on
an underpinning of fairly circumscribed middle-class
ideas. The platform from which his characters of
sense say their say on learning, love, and religion
seems ridiculously inadequate to all the folk who
dedicate their lives to gaining knowledge, to loving,
or to having faith. They reproach Molière for depriv-
ing us of all the indispensable values and giving us in
their place no more than sundry maxims. Such criticism is an outcome of the persistence with which
Molière's aphorisms are quoted in complete disregard
of the process whereby he invented them and of the
exigencies of his calling. It is one thing to incorporate
a wise point of view in a play and quite another to
make an intellectually satisfying statement of it, and
the two should be kept totally distinct. Henriette is
not a girl whose favors Molière has enjoyed and
whose charms he is ecstatically idealizing for us: she
is a girl whom he would have liked to know and has
never possessed save in daydream. This Ariste has
found no Léonor, and Célimène is not in a class with
Agnès. Bear in mind, too, that the ethical code of a
middle-class family of that period was an altogether
more serious affair, more substantial, more austere,
and more consonant with realities, than the values

current in worldly society, and that such a family as that in the play was to Molière an ideal that he had hardly managed to depict except in its outward appearances. And, finally, do not forget that a man who could formulate maxims embodying wisdom, or even mere common sense, in the midst of turmoils and miseries, harassments within and without, in frustration and sacrifice, is giving proof of no ordinary mettle. The greater exaltations are also the greater consolations. It is natural that we should be impelled to put the highest premium of all on his suffering. Gauge his own anguish by the scale of Clitandre's, or even of Chrysale's, and you contemplate something that can be called valor. Let any skeptic subject himself to an honest trial of the same ordeal.

We have seen that the exigencies of Molière's calling necessitated his thinking and seeing in sharp outlines. All debatable ideas, all ideas at loggerheads with society or in a merely formative stage, had to be assimilated, if they were to get across the footlights, to ideas already familiar, categorized—in short, obvious. Here was the reason for choosing, from among the ideas to be antagonized, those that were defective or ungenuine, that they might be set in contrast with the ideas that were accepted as valid. But these, more often than not, were bound up with traditional ways of dramatizing them, inasmuch as the memory telescopes experienced reality with the abstract idea underlying it; whence the proneness of comedy to look backward in time for its underpinning. Being simultaneously both case history and appraisal, comedy is conservative by the laws of its organization, whether after Molière's pattern or Aristophanes'.

In our contemplation of the seventeenth century we often become, it seems to me, the victims of an optical delusion. We mix up different periods, read unity into what was actually multifold, see as static what was evolving—all as Alceste did, and in pretty much Alceste's way. He started out believing in the perfectibility of man, or at least in man's attainment of a

higher level through conduct compounded of rationality and volition. The mankind of Descartes, Corneille, Poussin, and the Port Royal is a mankind self-
determined and self-made. Its ideal goal is complete-
ness, roundedness, as the crown of the attainable. But
recognition of man as he actually is, in all his muddle
and all his reflex motivation, comes to the fore in
those who would reform him. What they see is a
general anarchy; a clash between the pure aspirations
of religion and human selfishness; a Pascal who sees
nothing to choose between a godless mankind and
mankind according to Montaigne; a glare of light
thrown on themselves from minds both aroused and
illuminated by the ideal of rationality that actuates
them. Thus, on contact with the actualities and
through the coming-of-age of reason itself, the gulf
between reason and reality is exposed—reality the
plaything of blind forces; reason a mere form, gradu-
ally emptied of its content and becoming one more
of those imposing forms such as grammar and prosody
have erected after its likeness. Along toward the turn
of the century we discern everywhere this juxtaposi-
tion of reason and reality, not interpenetrating at all
but remaining as it were in suspension in each other's
presence.

Molière's life falls in the period of this development.
At the outset he was a professional man embarking on
his career with eager delight and equipped to get
ahead by decent and dexterous means. He used his
playhouses, his company of actors, and his fame to
make serious drama the richer by a humanity un-
adorned and soiled, its very core laid bare—the seamy
side of the painted scenery. But he had to breathe the
air of his own time. He had his art and his personal
life to nourish. He threw himself into bringing order
out of confusion, redeeming man from his corruption,
and in short raising the human level through comedy
as Corneille was doing through tragedy and Descartes
through analytical philosophy. The task was no trivial
one. Descartes and Corneille perceived a rationality in

things. Molière, like Pascal, perceived none. And, pre-
cluded from falling back on God, he could apprehend
no eternal truth underlying the outward aspects.
What was true was mankind as observed—no very
edifying sight. But this reality, this ignoble truth,
should be invested with an atmosphere of falsity by
virtue of the comic stratagem. Reason, shut out from
actuality, should stamp its pattern on actuality as a
means of reprehending its illogicality. By revealing
the senselessness of human behavior people should be
made to think that truth is something other than what
we see with our own eyes. But where is truth to be
sought? Molière waxes indignant; his logical protagonists hold forth; but reason never puts in an appearance save under the disguise imposed on affairs. The
depiction of distortions turns into a distorted depiction.

And yet Molière loved wisdom, loved rationality;
Alceste is there to prove it. Molière had the signal
merit of conceiving and upholding his simple and
exalted idea of mental health in the face of his own
history, his occupation, and the misunderstandings to
which he laid himself open. There were two men in
him: a canny though intensely emotional, reasonable
though muddled bourgeois who took charge in his
energetic and sanguine intervals; a clear-eyed cynic,
full of suppressed bitterness, who ruled his hours of
weariness and hopelessness. But he had no love for
cynicism, none for hopelessness. A core of strength
in him made his suffering more unendurable than it
would have been to another. And his judicial faculty
never gave in. This extremely moody and restive man
never put up with self-deception. Every time we set
out to change something in outer circumstance by
changing ourselves, every time we stake everything
on our passions in the feeling that we no longer have
anything to lose, every time we wilfully blind ourselves as a way of getting more light, Molière makes
us uncomfortable and stops us in our tracks; we might
well put it that he makes us look very small indeed.

But his method is unapproachable as a way of expos-
ing bogus improvement and bogus revolutions, of
condemning dogged self-love, of unmasking whatever
is incorrigible in the secret life of man and in his life
among his fellows. I doubt whether the most sensitive
or the most acute of us can contrive to perfect himself
in self-knowledge without Molière's help. If it were
compulsory to sum up his teaching, I should put it
that he teaches us the unspeakably difficult art of seeing ourselves in spite of ourselves. Illuminations of this
sort are of a quite different kind and quality from the
doctrine of the golden mean that is constantly being
dinned into our ears. Molière's doctrine could never
on any terms constitute a complete humanism; but no
conceivable humanism will ever be complete without
Molière.

The life lived with such valor was to end amid grim
hardships. In March 1672 Lully dealt Molière a formidable blow by securing to his Académie a monopoly
in music and ballet. The sums lately spent on refitting
the Palais Royal auditorium were rendered useless.
The rage for ballet being what it was, Molière's company was left without any hope of large-scale profits.
And the blow was especially grievous as coming from
the king. Louis XIV, though he had withdrawn from
dancing after *Britannicus* and *Les Amants Magnifiques*, was always enraptured by ballet performances.
Lully's new license deprived Molière of one of his
most reliable means of giving pleasure. It appears to
be inaccurate to say that the king had shown a lessen-
ing of enjoyment of Molière's comedies; but in accommodating Lully's wish he seems to have given the
right of way to a greater enjoyment. "Among the
royal advisers," Fustel de Coulanges has written, "Colbert stood for the hopes of public opinion, the necessity of order, and the passion for work; Louvois stood
for such ambitions as are natural to kingship—the
need of prestige, magnificence, renown. Louis XIV,
after several years' hesitation between the two men,
swung to Louvois's side." Would it be too fanciful to

rediscover the king's hesitation in the shows and public pleasures themselves?—to detect an analogy of the
same thing in a Molière devoted to order, rectifica-
tion, and work and a Lully who was sacrificing everything else to glitter and popularity? The dates would
correspond well enough. Of course, Molière had indis-
putably played Lully's present part himself; but Lully,
over and above all his other advantages, had a genius
for purveying the gaudy and superficial pleasure that
never exacts the taking of thought.

The Palais Royal actors, by protesting, won the
concession of twelve violins and six singers. With this
sketchy outfit they could not dream of putting on the
comedy ballet *Le Malade Imaginaire* at court. It was
played at the Palais Royal February 10, 1673, and
with success despite the reduction of the divertissement to a niggardly scale. Lully had made good his
legal rights.

Molière acting in *Le Malade Imaginaire* and all but
dying on the very stage—there we have a symbol so
overwhelming that it would appear to justify any
imaginative license whatever. But, precisely because
the symbol is too enticing, it is imperative to refrain—
to practice the same abstemiousness that Molière himself did, and to restore *Le Malade Imaginaire* to its
place in the historical framework of comedy. Comedy
as he practiced it was a great deal more than a discipline. It was an expression—the one authentic, exhaustive expression of the man. He did not comprehend himself, he did not attain self-awareness, save in
so far as he hit upon the comic formulation of his
meanings. Not by any means that he was incapable of
other kinds of self-awareness or of dramatizing the
other directions that his vital energy might have
taken; but the comic inventiveness was to him what
dialectic is to the logician, what the expression of
feeling is to the lyric poet. It was fulfillment—his
accounting for what his existence meant. But, you
object, Molière was a sick man and Argan nothing of
the kind? To be sure, but what invites comic apprais-

al is not the actual condition of the ill person: it is rather the effect of his agitated preoccupation with bodily health. An invalid on the comic stage can be nothing but imaginary, but there is nothing imaginary about the fear of death, about strangling in the desperation of clutching at life. It is all but certain that Molière well knew this desperation and had begun to succumb to it. His pulling himself up short, his self-correction and comic castigation have in this play the same purport as in *Le Misanthrope*. He creates Argan not so much to prosecute his business as to know himself and, in his characteristic idiom, to express himself.

Molière in this play is closely akin to Montaigne. His skepticism about medical knowledge greatly resembles Montaigne's about philosophical knowledge. He had long since become aware of the capital that comedy could make of medicine and medicos. Kept exceedingly well informed by the Mauvilain for whose son he had sought a favor in the third *Tartuffe* petition, he was aware that quite a proportion of the medical faculty declined to recognize latter-day physiological discoveries—particularly the circulation of the blood. He had direct observation of the physicians of the royal household—and it is notorious that the physicians of royal households are not invariably chosen from among the best. *Don Juan*, *L'Amour Médecin*, *Le Médecin Malgré Lui*, and *Monsieur de Pourceaugnac* all register an echo of amusing consultations between a shrewd doctor and an impatient patient. Molière's disease was one of those that are practically always fatal—a fact well calculated to bolster the skepticism of a man who had no faith, or who had lost his faith, in mere will power. And he knew to boot that doctors, like cuckolds, are always good for a laugh.

The loss of his second son at the age of one month, in October 1672, had hardly reinforced his trust in the art of medicine. From the circumstance of his having fathered a child at this time it has been inferred that he and his wife had had a reconciliation. It would

first have to be shown that before that reconciliation
they had been living physically apart. A child can be
born of a discordant marriage; furthermore, total dis-
cord is as rare as total harmony. A succession of spats
and makings-up, an alternation of estrangement and
fondness, the leverage of the senses, the unpredictable
surges of desire, the disarming effect of habit—these
are a closer approximation of real life than the theatrical sequence that has been conjured up by hindsight.
Armande had made Molière wretched; Molière had
made Armande wretched; the wall between them had
by no means been obliterated, but habituation
breached it at many points, and those who live in
everyday proximity to each other ultimately experience the calculable results of their nearness. Grimarest,
apparently pretty accurate whenever he brings in
Baron, shows us Molière on cosy terms with Armande
and confiding in her as if she were a dear friend of
long standing, or at least a long-standing sharer of his
existence.

Shaken by Lully's triumph, harassed by his disease,
his weariness, and his lack of opportunity to relax and
let himself go on living, Molière appears to have experienced at this time a sort of desperation. On February 17, while showing symptoms of considerable
feebleness, he said to his wife and Baron: "As long as
my life was compounded of pain and pleasure in
equal parts, I thought myself fortunate, but now that
I am overwhelmed with troubles and unable to look
forward to any intervals of contentment and release,
I see clearly that I must bow out. I can't hold out any
more in the face of pains and worries that give me not
a moment's respite." Armande and Baron begged him
to give up going to the theater for that day. "How
do you think I can do that?" he answered. "There are
fifty poor workingmen with nothing but their day
wages to live on; what are they going to do if there's
no play? I should blame myself if I let them go without a single day's food that I was perfectly able to
supply."

He told the players to be ready at four precisely; otherwise he should not act, and the money taken in would have to be returned. Molière managed to play the part of Argan through to the last curtain. To the last curtain he managed to extort laughter over the imbecilities of a character in a panic about the state of his health. But when it came to the ceremony in *Le Malade Imaginaire* he was seized with a convulsion while delivering the *Juro*. He covered this mischance under forced laughter.

"When the play ended," runs Grimarest's account, "he put on his dressing gown and went to Baron's dressing room. He asked Baron what people were saying about his play. Monsieur Baron replied that his plays were always happily successful when intimately studied, and that the oftener they were performed the more they were enjoyed. 'But,' he added, 'you seem to me sicker than you were a little while ago.' 'So I am,' Molière told him; 'I have a murderous chill.' Baron took hold of his hands, found them like ice, and put them into his own muff to warm them. He sent someone to hunt up Molière's bearers to take him home at once; and he stayed with the sedan chair himself to guard against any accident between the Palais Royal and the Rue de Richelieu, where Molière had rooms. As soon as he was in his bedroom Baron undertook to have him swallow some bouillon, of which Molière's wife always had a quantity on hand for herself; for no one could take better bodily care of herself than she did. 'Oh, no,' he said; 'that bouillon of my wife's is regular aqua fortis to me. You know all the ingredients she has put into it. Give me a little piece of Parmesan cheese instead.' La Forest brought it to him. He ate some of it with a little bread; then he had himself put to bed. He had been in bed only a minute or two when he sent to ask his wife for a pillow impregnated with a sleep-producing drug, which she had promised him. 'Anything that doesn't get inside me,' he said, 'I am willing to try, but the cures that have to be swallowed scare me. It wouldn't take much to do me out of the little life I have left.' A moment later he was taken with a paroxysm of coughing, and, having spat, he asked for a lamp. 'Here,' he said, 'is something new.' Baron, seeing the blood that he had discharged, let out a startled cry. 'Don't be scared,' Molière said to him; 'you've seen me spew out much more than that. Just the same,' he added, 'go and tell my wife she should come up.' He was left in the company of two of the nuns that regularly come to Paris to collect money during Lent; he had supplied these two with lodgings. They gave him, in these closing minutes of his life, all the spiritual help for which their benevolence could be called upon, and he gave them evidence of all the feelings of a good Christian and of all due resignation to God's will. It was in the arms of these two good sisters that he then breathed his last, strangled by the copious outpouring of blood from his mouth. So it was that his wife and Baron, when they had once more climbed the stairs, found him dead."

This account, whatever may be thought of the rest of the work, rings true. It is one of the very few biographical documents about Molière that can be presumed to be something more than appropriate inventions. And a fairly searching scrutiny of it is enough to let us make out, without overmuch romancing, the relationships of the great man with the two persons who were his nearest.

The usages of the Church refused burial in consecrated ground to actors who had failed to make an antemortem *amende honorable* in the presence of a priest. This was a ceremony that no actor omitted if there were time for it. "Mademoiselle" Molière, in her petition to the Archbishop, complained that the Saint Eustache priests—the priests of what became Molière's parish when he moved to the Rue de Richelieu, a little before his death—had refused to be bothered when a messenger went to fetch them. When a father confessor arrived from the Rue de Richelieu, whether willingly or under protest, Molière was already dead. The whole issue hinges on this delay. By canon law

Molière had no claim to consecrated ground. Louis XIV, appealed to by Armande and Baron, undoubtedly communicated his own feeling to the Archbishop, who decreed an inquest and immediately afterward sanctioned a nighttime funeral ceremony. On Tuesday, February 21, 1673, at nine in the evening, the funeral procession drew out of the Rue de Richelieu in the light of torches borne by Molière's friends. Four priests carried the coffin, which was of wood covered with a tapestry pall. Six children clad in blue carried wax tapers in silver candlesticks. In the street a crowd had gathered. Whether as a sop to ill will or as a concession to usage, Armande had a distribution of livres made to the spectators. At the gates of the cemetery of Saint Joseph, mystery takes over. The grave, "raised one foot above ground level," was located in the middle part of the cemetery, near the cross. Later on, an aged chaplain let fall disclosures strongly suggesting that Molière was buried, not in this grave, but in an unconsecrated section of that abode of the dead.

Louis XIV, toward the end of his reign, took pleasure in looking backward down the long vista. One day he asked Boileau who, in his judgment, had been the best writer of their age. Boileau unhesitatingly declared that it had been Molière. "I was not of that opinion," the king rejoined, "but you understand these things better than I do."

INDEX